Manifesting With the Moon

Enlightening Minds
Expanding Hearts
Empowering Souls

Jana Groscost

Pismo Beach, California. USA

Copyright © 2016 Jana Groscost. All rights reserved. No part of this book may be reproduced or transmitted in any means without the written permission of the author.

ISBN: 1539595102
EAN-13: 978-1539595106

The intent of the author is to provide information about the general nature of manifesting to be utilized as a self-help tool for your personal use. While all attempts have been made to verify information provided in this publication, the author assumes no responsibility for errors, omissions, or contrary interpretations of the subject matter herein. In practical advice books, there are no guarantees of success or results achieved. It is not to be used as a form of treatment for physical, emotional, medical problems, or financial advice. All readers are advised to seek services of competent professionals regarding physical, emotional, medical or financial advice.

Subjects include: manifesting, new moon, full moon, lunar cycles, astrology, Law of Attraction, personal development, emotional healing, chakras, vibration enhancement, spiritual development, essential oils, and more.

This book is dedicated to everyone
who wants to create a better life.

May you manifest a life filled with miracles!

Table of Contents:

Introduction	1
Manifesting	6
Manifesting with Lunar Cycles	15
Manifesting and Essential Oils	23
Astrological Signs and the Chakras	31
Aries New Moon	38
Libra Full Moon	46
Taurus New Moon	50
Scorpio Full Moon	56
Gemini New Moon	60
Sagittarius Full Moon	66
Cancer New Moon	70
Capricorn Full Moon	76
Leo New Moon	80
Aquarius Full Moon	87
Virgo New Moon	91
Pisces Full Moon	97
Libra New Moon	101
Aries Full Moon	107
Scorpio New Moon	111
Taurus Full Moon	117
Sagittarius New Moon	121
Gemini Full Moon	127

Capricorn New Moon	132
Cancer Full Moon	140
Aquarius New Moon	144
Leo Full New Moon	150
Pisces New Moon	154
Virgo Full Moon	161
Conclusion	165
References	166
About the Author	170
Additional Personal Notes	172

Introduction

THE MYSTERIES OF THE COSMOS have intrigued mankind for all of history. By exploring what is "out there" scientists have discovered the same "stuff" is within each of us. Carl Sagan, an astrophysicist said, "We are star stuff." Another astrophysicist, Neil deGrasse Tyson said, "We are comprised of the same elements that exist in the stars. The good thing about science is that it's true, whether you believe in it or not."

Most people spend much of their life unaware of the seemingly unrelated coincidences and subtle relationships in nature and how they personally correlate to us. But it's not a stretch when we consider that we are all made up of the same elements as the stars. It's kind of mind-blowing when you think about it.

It's a human characteristic to seek answers outside of ourselves since all of our senses direct us to experience the world from an external perspective. Our sight, hearing, ability to touch, smell and taste all help us experience the world. Just look at a baby and how everything goes in its mouth. We learn to process the world with our senses.

As we discover what is out there and how it relates to us we can also turn inward, exploring the vast unknown of what is inside each of us. Ultimately, we can learn to merge the outer and inner world as a united system versus independent components. As we integrate this philosophy we become the masters of our universe. We attune ourselves to the internal and external systems that exist, tapping into the subtle rhythms of nature. We begin to realize we are *all* an integral part of a bigger system. It is our life's work to determine how we fit in, and contribute to the whole.

The sun, the moon, and the stars are a part of the system that influences us. Obviously, if the sun didn't shine, no food could grow. Less obviously, the moon and the dark of night influence the hidden aspects of us. The subconscious and unconscious minds are affected by the moon. It influences our moods and fears.

The sun and moon both have a gravitational pull on the earth to keep the orbit balanced, as well as a gravitational pull between them. They each work as a system with earth. The gravity between the sun, moon and earth pull upon anything that isn't attached to the earth – namely water. It influences the ocean tides. Since we are primarily made up of water, our internal system is effected by the pull of gravity between the sun, moon, and earth.

Our bodies move with the rhythm of the lunar cycles, just like the ocean tides. It affects us in a variety of ways as the moon moves through the cycles from what is called a new moon to the full moon and back to the new moon. With each of these cycles, we can learn to work with their subtle energies to balance our inner and outer worlds. Through awareness of what we feel, we can fine tune our compass to master our thoughts, emotions and behavior.

These cycles are nothing new. They have been influencing us for thousands of years. Our ancestors knew how to work with the cycles and their natural rhythms. They created rituals to honor the change of the lunar cycles and the seasons. Over time we have no longer needed to attune to these natural rhythms to relay upon these cycles for survival. Now these cycles can be used to deepen our spiritual development and self-awareness. As we learn to align ourselves with the natural rhythms, we can learn to manage ourselves and our life's path more effectively. For example, with the first stage of the lunar cycle, called a new moon, it is a time of inception and beginning. We can initiate new projects, set goals, and begin new routines. There is more information about the lunar cycles coming up in the Manifesting with the Lunar Cycles chapter.

Many of us carry deep dreams within our hearts that take years or even lifetimes to achieve. While persistence helps us inch our way forward, it takes courage to go out on a limb and dive into unfamiliar territory to help us stretch, grow, overcome beliefs, emotional wounds, and behavior that limit our results.

Faith in realizing our goals can be a challenge. We want to believe we are worthy of achieving our goals, but sometimes life experiences leave us with a tarnished belief of entitlement that we deserve to receive something. For example, maybe we have experienced some sort of abuse, but we are a good person always doing charity work or caring for others, yet we don't seem to get what *we* want. For us to overcome this sense of entitlement, we need to summon Divine help to build bridges between healing past experiences, emotional wounds, and creating new internal programming that supports us in manifesting everything we desire. By consciously working with the lunar cycles, we can gain information about hidden aspects of ourselves, and learn about the influence the sun, moon, and planets have upon us. This information helps us make better choices, be more patient with ourselves, and dive into our hidden psyche.

A new lunar cycle begins about every 28½ days. The start of each cycle is influenced by other elements in the cosmos such as the sun and other planets. Each new cycle is also influenced by the various astrological signs that cast their unique flare into each lunar cycle.

Learning about the characteristics surrounding each lunar cycle supports our ability to create more of what we want. It's a process of self-discovery. We may have natural strengths during particular astrological cycles, where other cycles feel more challenging. We can learn to embrace the cycles that are difficult and help us unwind deep seated beliefs and emotions that keep us from evolving.

Using a manifesting journal is a powerful tool to identify patterns you want to resolve, emotions you may feel, and changes you want to make. Goals rarely take just a few weeks to achieve, so revisiting them each month breathes new life and affirms one's commitment in achieving them. Each month we may fine tune goals as new information arises, until we reach it. A manifesting journal helps us process what we notice so we see progress. When we are open to following our intuition, we allow our natural path to unfold.

How to use this book

This book is intended to be used as a guide to work with each of the lunar cycles through the course of the astrological year. It isn't meant to be read cover to cover.

The chapters related to each new moon provides insight and characteristics that correlate to the lunar cycle. This helps us learn what distinctive elements may affect us. We can attune to the natural currents and notice how that makes us feel. Since this process is a personal journey, various tools are recommended to help develop an ongoing practice that supports inner growth, and strengthens our connection to our higher-self. There are exercises to help set goals, develop affirmations or mantras, and suggestions for empowering questions.

With the full moon chapters, there is information about duality since the sun and moon are in opposite astrological signs. The full moon sometimes feels like we are getting pulled in two directions. The full moon is a time of release. It stirs up unresolved emotions and patterns that the moon is reflecting. There are recommended exercises to help release emotional wounds and replace them with conscious programming. Some of the information is repeated with the various cycles to create a conscious ritual of initiation (the new moon), and releasing emotional wounds and replacing them (the full moon). This practice of releasing and replacing emotions can be done at any time as they arise as necessary, not just with the full moon.

Within this book there are places to write about your new and full moon experiences. You may also want to have a separate lunar cycle journal to track your progress over the years. It is helpful to be able to look back through the years and see what has taken place.

Manifesting

THE SECRET TO MANIFESTING is no secret at all. Yet for centuries, people have been searching for some magic formula to help them understand how to create what they want.

The truth is we are *born* to create. We have been gifted with an imagination, an intellect, and an inner passion to achieve greatness. Experiencing happiness and a sense of purpose through expressing our unique talents and qualities is our inherent right. It's simply a natural state for humans. So what stops us from getting what we want?

Manifesting is the process of taking a goal or intention from an *idea or intangible* state and creating it in *physical or tangible* form. Many people set goals but often never reach them, becoming frustrated with the process and giving up. But there are underlying factors that prevent achieving goals. Understanding these factors and learning how to manage them is the key to manifesting what we want.

We are always in a state of creating, whether we realize it or not. Some of it is conscious but most of it occurs unconsciously. Mental confusion, emotional trauma, and spiritual distress influence each of us and our ability to create. Essentially we feel unworthy or undeserving to receive.

The components that affect our ability to manifest work as a system; although we can identify individual components, they work together and influence each other, and in turn affect the functionality of the whole system. Imagine an automobile engine. Each part is necessary but one damaged part may affect other parts, and stop the engine from functioning properly. The human body is a remarkable system. It differs from a car engine in its ability to adapt to our experiences and circumstances. Sometimes the system continues to function when one part is no longer working well or isn't getting what it needs.

Our body is affected by emotional reactions. Each time we experience an emotion there is a chemical reaction that occurs in the body. Some emotional reactions create toxins in the body. How do you feel when you are angry? Does your blood feel like it is boiling? Blood pressure increases when we are angry or upset. How do you feel when you see a kind act? It may invoke tears of compassion, love, and joy. This is caused by the release of serotonin, the "feel good" hormone, into our system.

Emotions are initially processed in a part of the brain called the amygdala. This part of the brain determines if we are in danger and need to flee, or the emotions need to go to other parts of the brain for further processing. Although we may not have the same level of fear for survival as our cave dwelling ancestors did, we often get caught in a stress cycle because of emotional wounds we still hold.

When a person experiences traumatic events, their body continues to function at a less optimal level. The memory of events become ingrained in our cells. The cells are literally programmed by our thoughts and emotions. We process current experiences through filters based upon past situations and emotions. We fear a new experience will be something similar to what we have felt before. Thus we react because we don't want to feel that way again. Fears from emotionally traumatic events change our body's chemistry. It clouds our ability to accurately process information. By resolving emotional wounds and misperceptions our system can become whole again. Allowing us to hold more light, and enhances the ability to manifest.

Simple mindfulness about our thoughts heightens our awareness and ability to create more. Our thoughts create invisible messages that are carried far beyond the confines of our brain. The vibration of conscious and unconscious thoughts are projected into the Universe. They are like *e-mail* or energetic mail. Consistent thoughts we send into the cosmos are reflected by to us by the Universe. This is called the Law of Attraction – and the basis of what we *magnetize or attract* to us. We attract the same vibration we are projecting.

The Law of Attraction works equally for everyone without determining our true desires or intentions. The universe simply reflects back to us the frequency or message we are projecting. For example, if the goal is to receive more money but we believe we only feel we deserve a specific amount, manage money poorly – or whatever the core beliefs are – we'll continue to attract opportunities to *restrict the flow of money*. The emotions behind each belief influences our ability to manifest. It comes from within and is based upon whatever we consistently think, feel or believe. Most people never realize their thoughts are influencing and defining their results. Learning to unlock the fears and other subliminal blocks opens up a new path for success.

There is a simple formula for manifesting:

$$M^3 = \text{Magnify} + \text{Magnetize} = \text{Manifest}$$

Whatever we think about most often is *magnified*. What we *magnify* we attract or *magnetize* to us and this becomes what is *manifested*.

If we're creating undesirable results, it's worth the effort to look into the unconscious components to determine what aspects of our mental, emotional, and spiritual beliefs are affecting us. We need to plug the energetic leaks such as fears and incorrect beliefs, and learn to channel our energy towards what we want.

When we learn to let go of mental waste and obsolete emotions, our heart can expand, allowing the natural flow of abundance. Then it is possible to develop inner courage and take charge of our life so we create what we want. Once the unconscious elements that governed our life are removed through conscious choices, opportunities arise to work with our life's purpose. Mindful practices remove the power of the unconscious patterns and habits. As we let our talents shine, we liberate ourselves from thinking small and doubting our abilities. As we succeed, we inspire people around us to find courage and express their potential.

Each person experiences the healing and growth process differently. Ultimately, each of us is responsible for resolving the unconscious elements that influence us. There are numerous resources available to help us understand ourselves better, but without actively participating in our own process and implementing healing steps, our evolution suffers.

No one can heal us except ourselves. *When we are willing to remove all the elements that short-circuit the connection between us and the Divine (God, Spirit, the Universe or whatever name you choose to give the Higher Power), the more likely we are to create an everlasting flow of abundance in all areas of life.* When we consciously co-create, we choose to heal and resolve all areas of our life where we've lost power. True healing begins when we reclaim our power. Once we resolve the unconscious pattern we will:

- ➢ Remove misperceptions that cloud judgment
- ➢ Release barriers that break us down
- ➢ Invoke creative forces that easily sustain life
- ➢ Grasp fresh ideas that manifest success

Each time we make conscious choices, we move closer to understanding our own divinity – that part of us which assists in birthing new creations. Success in manifesting gets easier as our vibration aligns with what we want.

Imagine how life will change as we become more conscious of the influences that restrict our success. Once those factors are removed our results change, and we attract what we want.

Act as if...

I first heard the phrase *"act as if"* about 20 years ago. It was a part of a class about the Law of Attraction, which at the time was a new concept to me. The class included exercises in which we were to "act as if" something had already occurred or that we had received, even if we hadn't. We were to imagine what it felt like to live in the dream house, or drive the new car, or work at the ideal job. Visualization and journaling exercises were a part of the class.

It's funny I had used these types of exercises without even realizing the impact. I would walk through houses I liked just to get a feel of what it would be like to live there. Or I would go to stores to get a feel for a car, furniture, clothes, or whatever I wanted. I would talk with the sales people *as if* I was going to purchase it. They assumed I had money to buy it because I spoke with confidence. I believed that there would be a way for me to get whatever I really wanted. I remember saying to myself, "If there's a will, there's a way."

Our will plays a big part in getting anything. If there isn't passion around a goal, then we most likely won't reach it.

I also used these techniques to envision myself receiving a college degree, landing a particular job, or reaching health related goals. Whatever I wanted I implanted a seed in my subconscious and tapped into the feelings behind being, doing, or getting anything.

The "act as if" phrase has become mainstream. This concept is a big part of manifesting our goals. The more we can engage the subconscious and all of our senses, the more likely we are to get what we focus on.

Now I engage in these types of activities to manifest everything I desire; whether it's arriving at my destination on time, breezing through traffic, having a new register open at a busy store, optimizing my health, enhancing my relationships, overcoming fears and difficult situations, or whatever I want. I not only visualize, but *feel* my desired outcome before it happens.

The concept behind the "act as if" phrase is more than just believing in getting what we want, it's about confidently moving towards the goal knowing the Universe supports us. It's easy for the conscious mind to discount something that doesn't currently exist, but we need to override the logic as to *how* we will get it, and turn that over to the Universe to create. It is living a faith-based life versus an evidence-based life. Often the term "faith" is related to religion, but in manifesting this term encompasses an even broader spectrum.

Manifesting is a faith-based process. We want things to be different. But in order for things to be different, we need to act "as if" they are different. Otherwise, we continue to create the same results. Our inner wisdom speaks to us in subtle synchronicities. Your job is to follow the quiet coincidence that lead you towards the goal.

"Acting as if" isn't about *hoping* things will be better, but then *worrying* nothing will change. In this situation, fear is the underlying vibration. "Acting as if" is a tool to engage all of the senses so the subconscious has a frame of reference for what we want.

The subconscious can't reason. It simply accepts everything that is repeatedly impressed upon it. I'm sure you can think of many situations or beliefs that were ingrained as a child that simply aren't true. Often, when we set goals, conscious reasoning or programming steps in to say, "Sure, but how am I going to do or get that?" Many people never get started because they don't know or can't understand the entire process. The conscious mind wants to know all the steps. But we don't need to know *how* to reach our goals. We just need to take the first step that is in front of us. The first synchronicity will lead to another clue. As we find clues, other steps will be revealed when it's time. When we disengage the conscious mind from the manifesting puzzle, we allow the subconscious mind to find creative solutions that have no limitations like the conscious mind. The subconscious will look for solutions to make whatever we believe true. I love using empowering questions. I would say something like, "Why is it so easy for me to have a booked client schedule?" Then my subconscious goes to work, helping me see how easy it is to get clients. To get what we want, we first need to visualize ourselves having it or believing we deserve it.

We are in a position to make choices that change our programming. We are capable of dreaming our life into reality by consciously training ourselves to get whatever we want. By "acting as if" we see ourselves finishing the big race, winning the game, landing the job, buying the house, traveling the world, we consciously reprogram ourselves. It's up to us to overcome the fears and unconscious programming through "acting as if" exercises.

Each new moon chapter has a section dedicated to writing out goals "as if" they have already occurred. Use words such as "I have," "I am," "We went" or other words in the present or past tense instead of future words such as "I will". Be descriptive, engage all the senses, and share your experience on these pages or in a journal "as if" the goal has been reached.

By doing this, the subconscious will look for ways to make it true. It believes the reality we create in our minds. I have sometimes tell my clients to "lie" to themselves to create their reality. The conscious mind knows we don't currently have what we want, so we must override the conscious efforts that keep us from getting whatever we want.

In addition to writing out your goals "as if" they have occurred, share them with someone. Find a manifesting partner with whom you can talk about your goals openly as if they have been reached. Listen to your manifesting partner talk about their goals. Make sure they understand the process as well so they don't put a damper or judgement on anything. Recording the goals or messages is a good way to get it into the subconscious. Hearing our own voice is a powerful way to program the subconscious. However, you choose to document and engage the process, remember to have fun. Everyone's manifesting process is different. I often get asked, "What is the best formula or method for manifesting?" I always tell them, "Whatever system or practice you will actually do." It's an active, exploratory process that can be fun and exciting.

Manifesting with the Lunar Cycles

THE MOON IS CONSTANTLY CHANGING, reflecting our emotions, needs and moods. We enhance our ability to manifest and understand ourselves better by learning to work with nature's rhythms; and the lunar cycles are one way to do it.

The moon and earth have a gravitational pull between them. The ocean tides are created as a result of this pull. We are also influenced by the gravitational pull because we are comprised of over sixty percent water. Our bodies move with the rhythm of the lunar cycle and tides.

The night sky represents the parts of us that are unseen or unknown. As the moon moves through its various cycles it illuminates the unseen parts of us, helping us understand ourselves better.

Our emotions are part of the hidden aspects that are brought to light with the cycles of the moon. Learning about the phases of the moon and astrological signs are tools to assist us in understanding the ebb and flow of life. These subtle currents that influence our lives can be enhanced by understanding the characteristics of the astrological sign the moon is moving through. The more attune we are into our inner world and natural flow the more successful we are going to be in reaching our goals.

Astrologers divide the lunar month into eight cycles and give some recommendations on how to work with each one:
- ▽ New Moon – Dreaming
- ▽ Crescent Moon – Beginning
- ▽ First Quarter Moon – Manifesting
- ▽ Gibbous Moon – Perfecting
- ▽ Full Moon – Illuminating
- ▽ Disseminating Moon – Sharing
- ▽ Last Quarter Moon – Evaluating
- ▽ Balsamic Moon – Surrender

The moon is constantly reflecting our emotions back to us. As the light of the moon changes each night it reflects and stirs up emotions that need to be acknowledged, addressed, and resolved.

Emotions are a part of the hidden aspect of us that is influenced by the lunar cycles. Emotions are waves of energy and hold a specific vibration that should be fluid and move through the body.

Unfortunately, many stuck emotions resulted from experiences when we were children and ill-equipped to manage the emotions. Without tools to properly process or manage emotions, we buried, ignored, or denied them so that we would not have to feel them. The *fear* of feeling painful emotions again actually causes us to attract situations where we feel similar emotions until we learn how to resolve the original experiences. The moon helps us to understand and resolve these emotions by bringing them to light. Once emotional wounds are resolved we no longer hold those vibrations and we can process life from a different perspective.

Working with the lunar cycles helps us tap into the rhythm of life. Instead of setting an annual intention, we set monthly ones. It creates a flow because we revisit existing goals to fine tune them, or seed new ones with the new lunar cycle. Creating a monthly ritual such as writing down intentions and visualizing them embeds them in the subconscious. When we write down a goal, we are more likely to achieve it.

New Moon – Dreaming

When the *new moon* takes place there is no visible moon. The night sky is dark and there is a sense of inner stillness. Emotions are at their lowest levels of the lunar cycle, which makes it the perfect time to set new goals, begin new projects, or initiate agreements.

With the new moon, the sun and moon are unified in their influence upon us. Both are affected by the same astrological sign. This is the dream time. Anything we can imagine we can achieve. The subconscious mind cannot distinguish between truth and a lie. It simply accepts everything that is continuously impressed upon it. It's a good way to consciously program ourselves.

It is a perfect time to set intentions and visualize success. Beginning the cycle with some visualization exercises or meditation are powerful tools to help change our reality.

First Quarter – Beginning

As the light of the moon is increasing, there is an opening to new possibilities. Now is the time to begin looking outside ourselves for support in achieving goals. The time between the new moon and the first quarter is the *action* stage. It's building momentum and getting things going. Be attuned to inspired action that is beyond the perceived plan. Follow subtle synchronicities that are clues from your inner wisdom and guide the flow.

The sun and the moon are at right angles with each other; in astrological terms this is known as a "square." Squares mean change.

During this phase, minor adjustments may be made related to the new moon intentions. It's a good time to determine *why* we want to achieve the goal. Do you understand what is motivating you to reach these goals? Is your motivation based on supporting desires of the ego or true power?

Notice any personal resistance that may arise during this time as changes are being made. We often sabotage our results by procrastinating or avoiding necessary action. Resistance is a form of fear. As we push against longstanding beliefs, fears around feeling unworthy to receive what we want commonly crop up. Since we constantly have the opportunity to change, fear could be an acronym that debilitates us – *Forget Everything And Run* or it could be an acronym which motivates us – *Face Everything And Rise*. The choice is always up to us. However, it helps to have tools in place to help overcome moments when fears arise.

Visualization, meditation, prayer, affirmations, essential oils, energy work, and revisiting motivation in achieving the goals are a potent way to help stay on track with the process.

Full Moon – Illuminating

Full moons show us how to use the complementary energies of opposite astrological signs. They help us become aware of hidden aspects of ourselves, and see the world through different perceptions. While the Sun symbolizes the masculine spirit of focus, intention, consciousness and self awareness, the moon symbolizes the feminine spirit, growth, change, decay, death, and rebirth.

As the light of the moon increases and reaches its peak with the full moon, energy and momentum are intensifying. This time of high energy stimulates great productivity. During this phase there is a culmination of elements that have come together to move our new moon intentions forward. When intentions are not fully realized at this time, the full moon highlights fears and emotions that we need to address.

It illuminates incorrect beliefs, patterns, and emotional wounds that stand between us and what we want. The full moon brings in new perspectives, breakthroughs, and epiphanies. These are clues to help us achieve the new moon intentions. There are also shifts in perceptions that differ from the initial new moon intentions as new insight is reflected with the full moon.

At the time of the full moon, the sun and moon are in opposite astrological signs. Think of it like balancing two sides of a scale. The sun is on one side of the scale and the moon on the other. For example, when the sun is in Capricorn, the moon is in Cancer – the opposite sign of Capricorn. Both of these astrological signs influence us based upon their unique characteristics. This is one reason it is important to learn the characteristics of both astrological signs to understand what potential issues could arise, and create balance between the two scales. In this case, Capricorn represents how we take physically care for ourselves, our career, and how we project ourselves in the world, while Cancer focuses on how we feel, nurture ourselves, and compassion.

While the new moon is a time of introspection and internal review, the full moon influences us through external sources. It affects us through the actions, emotions, and beliefs of other people. Whatever needs to be resolved within us is reflected to us through other people and situations. Take note of people who stir up emotions.

It's a good time to pause and be aware when someone or something sets off an emotional response. These are clues that something within us needs to be addressed or resolved. With the full moon people reflect our issues, yet we typical respond by judging or blaming them instead of looking inward.

Emotions run high as the water within the body is pulled by the opposition of the sun and moon. This causes us to be more emotional. When we are more emotional, our lens is out of focus on how we perceive situations and may react more abruptly. If we can briefly pause before reacting, we can learn to identify what we feel. It provides a prime time to resolve lingering emotions and release them. Through awareness of our hidden emotions and learning to resolve them, we purify ourselves and align with our intentions.

Use rituals that are symbolic, personal, and relate to "letting go" – such as writing down a list of emotions describing toxic people and situations in our life and then burning the list. The smoke symbolically carries away the intentions. This helps release anything that no longer serves us and enhances the purification process. This exercise can be done physically or during visualization exercises.

In addition to smoke, water is a powerful purifier. Using water as a cleanser can be a physical experience such as taking an Epsom salt bath or shower, or figurative such as visualizing swimming or rinsing away toxins under a waterfall. The water can melt away emotions, patterns, beliefs and anything else that we wish to remove.

Last Quarter – Evaluating

Between the full moon and last quarter is an extended time to release, remove, and resolve. We may need to remove toxic people, and resolve and release emotional wounds to provide a clear channel for what we want. This eliminates static – such as misperceptions about ourselves and others, providing a cleansing of unnecessary emotional clutter. Since the light of the moon is receding, it's a reminder to dive deeper – shedding habits, emotions, and conditioned responses.

Again, when we reach the last quarter point of the lunar cycle, the sun and the moon are at right angles with each other. In astrological terms this is known as a "square." Squares mean change. There may be an awkward feeling as there is a shift into unfamiliar territory. Having faith in ourselves and trusting in the process, is the remedy to navigate difficult changes.

As the moon's light decreases, we may feel like drawing within to concentrate on completing necessary tasks to achieve desired results. We may have a sense of harvesting as goals come to fruition. There may be significant milestones that have been met during this cycle as we move inward and prepare for another new moon.

Manifesting and Essential Oils

ESSENTIAL OILS ARE THE NATURAL AROMATIC compounds found in the flowers, bark, seeds, and other parts of plants. These aromatic essences provide protection for the plant against disease and predators. We all have experienced essential oils – whether we are walking by a lavender plant, rubbing mint leaves, or peeling an orange.

Essential oils have been used throughout history for their aromatic qualities, medicinal, and therapeutic benefits. They were used in ancient rituals for thousands of years. Some essential oils such as frankincense were considered more precious than gold. Because of the expense in obtaining frankincense. It was often only available for royalty.

In recent years, essential oils have become more popular as people learn about their health promoting properties. The chemical compounds in the plants oils provide a fast, safe, and effective way to support us physically and emotionally. They help us naturally support our moods, emotions, and stress.

Integrating essential oils into a wellness practice is a tangible tool that helps us release emotional wounds. It's simple, and everyone can learn how to use them. Releasing emotional wounds helps us raise our vibration and we attract new opportunities and stuff to us.

In 1989 scientists discovered that our emotions are stored in a part of the brain called the amygdala gland. This gland is located in the brain and plays a significant role in storing and releasing emotional trauma. It is the gatekeeper through which all sensory information is processed. When we have an experience or information comes in, the amygdala determines if it needs to be sent to the adrenal glands first, for a fight or flight response, or onto other parts of the brain for further processing.

The amygdala is programmed to react without the benefit of input from the logical brain. Studies at New York University proved this gland does not respond to sight, sound, or touch, it only responds to our sense of smell. Through our sense of smell we have the ability to release emotional wounds and trauma stored in the amygdala. Essential oils can help release emotional wounds that have caused longstanding painful memories and limit our ability to manifest.

Many psychologists believe that most of our emotional programming and patterns are determined before age seven. As a child, we lacked the emotional maturity to understand our feelings. On some level, our ego felt our needs were not being met, creating fear that our survival was at risk. Sounds extreme doesn't it? For example, a toddler is left crying in her crib, feeling neglected because her mom is sleeping off a migraine. The child feels abandoned because no one is picking her up. These types of hidden patterns and fears end up being the unconscious limitations that stand between us and creating flourishing relationships, balanced health, and financial abundance.

In my metaphysical coaching practice, I look at a client's physical issues as a symbolic representation of emotional issues. I believe emotions are the catalyst for physical issues that break down and create disruptions in our body's energy system, or *dis-ease*.

When there are consistent thoughts or beliefs (conscious or unconscious) about ourselves we create an energetic imprint in our body. It affects the neurons in the brain and chemical reactions that can change our DNA. This may cause a short circuit or breakdown in the flow of energy in the body. As such, it often appears as physical ailments in the body. Since we are magnetic beings we attract vibrations that support what we are projecting – more opportunities to feel abandoned, abused or rejected. When we subconsciously feel unworthy, we attract situations where we feel incapable or inadequate. This can physically show up in the body in many different ways, such as stomach disorders, ulcers, acid reflux, or other digestive issues because we have difficulty processing life (processing food). As we make the correlation between the physical body and what we feel we can make conscious choices to change our thoughts, beliefs, and behavior that have caused the body's breakdowns.

Over the past two decades, it has been an interesting journey for me learning how the body works and how essential oils support us. Each time we feel an emotion there is a chemical reaction that occurs. With essential oils, we can offset the flood of toxins that may occur with certain emotional reactions. Essential oils are more than just something that smells good. Our blood chemistry changes as a result of using them. They help us feel calmer, elevate our mood, and other responses.

Our body's chemistry has an impact on every cell in our system. It can positively and negatively influence us, and even cause changes in our DNA. When someone does something nice for us, we do something nice, or we witness a random act of kindness our serotonin levels increase. Serotonin helps us feel good. Essential oils such as wild orange, lemon, and lime have a similar effect on our body's chemistry. They are uplifting. Essential oils such as lavender or frankincense can be soothing to the nervous system, helping us relax and feel less stressed. Memory and alertness may be enhanced by smelling essential oils such as rosemary and peppermint. Applied along the spine, peppermint has a cooling sensation on a hot summer night.

In addition to raising our vibration by assisting us in resolving emotional wounds, essential oils can be used to anchor affirmations, goals, and setting empowering questions. Our sense of smell is the most powerful sense we have. Do you recall a situation where a smell takes you back to a particular time or place? My mom loved to bake. In the fall, she made pumpkin chocolate chip cookies, and the whole house smelled like pumpkin, cinnamon, and clove. Now whenever I smell cinnamon and clove it reminds me of helping her plop cookie dough on the baking sheets. The body can also recall smells that we associate with painful memories. We have been *unconsciously* programmed by smells. Why not use them to create what we want?

We can *consciously* program what we want by breathing in the essential oil while we reciting affirmations, visualizing achieving a goal, or asking empowering questions. Then whenever we smell the essential oils we used to program ourselves, the brain subconsciously remembers the connection between the smell and our affirmation, goal or empowering question. I love using wild orange with manifesting because it elevates our mood. Wild orange trees are abundant with fruit. They overflow with the fruit and symbolically these trees remind us that life is abundant and the Universe freely gives to all of us. The Universe doesn't discriminate nor determine who should receive and who should not. The sun shines equally on saints and sinners. It simply gives to everyone who believes they deserve to receive all the goodness it provides. The key to manifesting is removing any limiting beliefs that stand between us and what we want.

A few years ago, I had asked the Universe to provide me with tools to help people heal more quickly. I had no idea what would happen. Within the next few months a friend asked me to try some essential oils she had been using. I had been using essential oils for about 15 years so this wasn't something new. But she told me these essential oils were different than any she had used. I was skeptical because I had used so many different ones over the years. She was right. I remember opening the bottles and thinking, "Wow, these oils are different." The smell was more pure, intense, and potent, just like the actual plant was in front of me.

I've learned that not all essential oils are created equal. It is an unregulated industry so companies can deceive us by saying their essential oils are "pure, organic, or therapeutic," yet their oils may be a lower grade, include filler oils, or synthetic. Lower grade products lead to less effective or no results.

I had used essential oils in a few classes I taught prior to these new ones, but I didn't notice a difference. But when I used these new essential oils I had such a profound shift that I knew I needed to share them with others.

My experience with these essential oils may be different that of other people. And I respect their desire to use other brands of oils. But, as a holistic intuitive practitioner, I knew dōTERRA's essential oils were here to work through me. It's a tangible tool that anyone can learn to work with and helps them balance their body's chemistry.

Our internal chemistry affects all aspects of our body, including the building blocks in the cells, our DNA. Unresolved emotions cause a breakdown in the DNA. That programming is carried forward through the generations until someone chooses to break the cycle. That means that any unresolved emotions that affected our ancestors is a part of our DNA. We have the choice to continue with the current pattern and transfer it to our children, or we can stop the pattern by resolving our emotional wounds, as well as releasing our ancestor's emotional wounds.

Doctors know there is a relationship between our family's health and our health. They may not make the connection between the emotional piece and our health. But ongoing studies are seeing this correlation, and as more studies are done, it will eventually become common knowledge.

Holding onto consistent emotions such as anger, resentment, jealousy, guilt or shame create chemical reactions that may break down the body. These lower vibrating emotions short circuit our system. We can offset emotional reactions by using essential oils. By opening up a bottle and breathing it in, our blood chemistry begins to change. We can also shift lower vibrating emotions through mindfulness practices. Go to www.ManifestingEssentials.com under the Mindfulness tab to experiment with these types of exercises.

Plants support us by holding a vibration that helps us heal. Do you feel attracted to certain plants, maybe a type of tree, or flower? In our humanness it is difficult to hold a consistent vibration. We go through a range of emotions. Situations trigger emotions or fears, people and situations throw us off balance, and there are underlying emotional issues that are hidden in our psyche that cause our vibe to be volatile. We can take a walk in the park or nature to help calm us down. Or we can open a bottle of an essential oil and quickly change how we feel.

There are more medical studies being performed using essential oils and how they affect us. The correlation between releasing emotional wounds and using essential oils is an effective and easy way to manage our wellbeing. Since resolving emotional wounds is a key part to raising our vibration so we attract what we want, I thought, "Great here is an awesome tool that people can learn how to use for their healing." It's empowering. My clients no longer only rely upon me helping them release emotional wounds. As people become more aware of the emotions they are feeling or physical issues in their body, they can look to essential oils to manage their physical and emotional health.

Here are a couple of suggestions on how to use essential oils to enhance manifesting and emotional healing. You can use them prior to meditation, prayer, or yoga. They may enhance spiritual connection, provide relaxation, or stop the monkey mind. Use a few drops in an Epsom salt bath for relaxation. Add them to a massage treatment.

As we deepen our connection with our higher-self, we receive greater guidance from our Divine source. Place a drop in your hands, rub them together, and take a couple of deep breaths. As you work through each new and full moon, try a few essential oils to help you set your intentions, anchor affirmations, and release emotional wounds. Of course, there is much more information about essential oils. This provides a brief overview of how and why to use them in relationship to manifesting.

For those of you who are new to using essential oils or have used less effective essential oils, I encourage you to contact me for more information about them. The essential oils I recommend are from a company called dōTERRA – which is Latin for "Gift of the Earth." I find these essential oils are very different and have enhanced my life by helping me manage stress levels and emotions. They have also helped my client's learn how to feel more empowered. They are an effective tool to help us release emotional wounds, anchor affirmations, and feel more inspired.

My intention is to provide tools to enlighten people's minds, expand people's hearts, and empower people's souls. My website has blog posts, podcasts, videos, and a free e-course available to help you learn more about essential oils and manifesting – visit my site at www.ManifestingEssentials.com. I want people to feel empowered with their lives, and learn how to manage their health. Contact me through my website to learn how to integrate essential oils into your spiritual practice and wellness routine.

Astrological Signs and the Chakras

THE SANSKRIT WORD CHAKRA literally translates to mean a wheel or disk. These are the energy centers in our body where energy flows or moves. Although we may not be able to physically see these we can learn to sense them or learn when we are experiencing imbalances within them.

Although there are dozens of energy centers on and around the body, there are seven primary chakras that are located from the base of the torso to the crown of the head. These can be imagined as swirling funnels of energy, sort of like a cyclone, which funnels information, gathers energy, and brings information on an unconscious level into the body for processing.

Each of the seven main chakras connects with various physical aspects of the body, such as nerves, glands, and major organs. For example, the first chakra governs the organs of elimination such as the kidneys, skin, colon and other issues discussed in the Aries New Moon chapter. The second chakra governs issues related to the ovaries, testicles, bladder, kidneys, and large intestine. The third chakra governs the stomach, spleen, liver, pancreas, lower esophagus, and middle spine. The fourth chakra governs the heart and lungs. The fifth chakra governs the upper lungs, thyroid, and throat. The sixth chakra governs the sinuses, face, ears, eyes, nose, and nervous system. The seventh chakra governs the nervous system and the brain.

Since energy is fluid and moving, it's essential that our chakras remain open as clear channels to process information. When there are blockages due to emotional wounds, energy cannot flow freely. This clog causes energy to stagnate and potentially breaks down the organ or physical function associated with that chakra.

For example, a woman who had an argument with her husband develops laryngitis. The woman, feeling unheard, shuts down emotionally. The laryngitis symbolizes her inability to speak and be heard. In this case, the throat chakra has been affected. If she realizes the connection between her frustration in communicating and feeling unheard, and honors the process, then she can release the tension in her throat and recover from the physical ailment.

Keeping the chakras open and aligned can be difficult. We are constantly bombarded with energy and often never realize it. Therefore, we need tools to help us learn when there are imbalances as well as how to rebalance them. The chakras can be balanced using different tools such as color, music/sound, breath work, food, crystals, essential oils, visualization, and other tools. Try different tools or combinations of tools to find what works best for you.

In 2009 I saw a correlation between music, the twelve astrological signs, and the twelve major/minor chakras on the torso. Nature has a magnificent way of weaving information together in seemingly random arrangements that have a pattern that is symbolic and orderly. Learning how to "sense" various relationships helps us understand ourselves and the subtle energies that influence us.

There have been studies done with light waves that are influenced by a particular musical note being played. The light wave that is created has a color associated with it, which in turn has been used to determine the color associated with each chakra. We are attracted to certain colors and sounds that help us feel a certain way such as uplifted, calm, energized, etc. and repelled by others that sound like nails on a chalk board and colors that make us feel chaotic or stressful. I have been playing with this concept and find it fascinating.

Although we talk about the chakras as being independent, they work as a system. Technically we could look at each of the astrological signs and find characteristics that link them to several different chakras. For example, Capricorn can be associated with the root chakra whose function supports our survival and security. Capricorn expresses itself in how we make a living and financially take care of ourselves. Capricorn could also relate to the second chakra in following our passion to take care of ourselves. There are also characteristics relating Capricorn to the third chakra and how we stand in our power and express authority. This too could also be an argument that Capricorn relates to the fifth chakra (throat) in expressing our desires. Finally, Capricorn could be represented in the Third Eye (6th chakra) as the ever present desire to reach the highest point in our humanness – enlightenment.

For the scope of this book I relate the chakras with the twelve astrological signs and the twelve musical notes in an octave. Although there is information that astrological signs relate to chakras different than I am demonstrating, I feel the need to honor the information I have been presented with and use it to demonstrate the correlations between the chakras, musical notes, and astrological signs.

As a musician I learned that Middle C is the center point on the piano. There are seven primary keys (white keys) between middle C and high C, and five sharp or flat keys (black keys) between the seven primary keys. These twelve keys create what is called an octave.

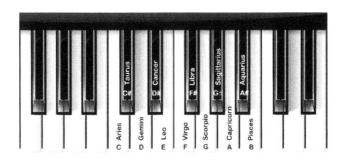

Aries is the first sign of the astrological year. I will therefore relate it to the musical note Middle C. Aries relates to "who we are." This also corresponds to the first chakra in creating stability, security, and fulfilling our basic needs.

Taurus relates to our values, what sustains us, our desires, motivation, and fears. It relates to the musical note C# (sharp) which corresponds to the chakra located half way between the base and sacral chakras. Relating this to the sexual chakra seems valid because sex is a strong motivator in our physical humanness.

Gemini relates to expressing our desires and uses thought, communication, and connecting with other people to expand ourselves. It relates to the musical note D which corresponds to the second chakra, the sacral chakra.

Cancer represents the womb, or place of gestation and inner growth. It relates to the musical note D# and is located between the second and third chakra. It helps us see the dual nature of life. Cancer is a creative matrix and contains the powers of creation and destruction.

Leo is where our personal power lies. The lion is the king of the jungle and has nothing to fear. It relates to the musical note E and is located at the third chakra, the Solar Plexus. The Solar Plexus represents the ability to stand in our power and fully express ourselves. The lower chakras relate to earthly connection and survival. When emotional wounds have been resolved, we no longer focus on survival issues but move into higher realms of life. The fourth through seventh chakras represent these higher planes.

Virgo relates to our ability to listen to our soul's voice. Virgo relates to the musical note F and is located at the heart chakra. It relates to the lower heart in connecting heaven to earth. Ultimately to become efficient we need to learn to listen to our inner wisdom. She also teaches us discernment – the ability to listen to our inner wisdom and sharpen our perceptions.

Libra helps us find balance. It relates to the musical note F# and is located at the thymus gland, between the heart chakra and throat chakra. The thymus bland absorbs higher frequencies from outer space (Libra is an air sign) and then shares it with the heart. It enhances our ability to make peace with ourselves and other people. The thymus gland is also the center of our immune system. One of the most powerful ways to awaken the immune system is to do what you love. Gently tap on the thymus gland while applying essential oils to the area are a great way to stimulate the gland and the immune system.

Scorpio helps us strip away our false beliefs and values. It relates to the musical note G and is located in the throat chakra. The throat is our source of verbal expression and ability to speak our highest truth. Scorpio helps us cut away any fluff and get to the truth of ourselves.

Sagittarius represents the ability to dream on a higher level. It relates to the musical note G# and is located at the zeal point which is located at the base of the brain stem. This chakra serves an important function in helping us manifest our Divine purpose. Sagittarius helps us expand our vision through enthusiasm, optimism, and its adventurous nature.

Capricorn represents our penetrating spiritual vision and achieving the highest destination. It relates to the musical note A and corresponds to the Third Eye chakra. The Third Eye is located between the eyebrows. It is our center of intuition. We may have an intuitive sense about something but may not choose to listen or heed warnings. Capricorn gives us a picture of the human being rooted to the earth, but free-scaling the heights of worldly ambition and spiritual aspiration.

Aquarius reflects our ability to pour knowledge and wisdom over the collective consciousness. It relates to the A# note and corresponds to the pineal gland. The pineal gland helps us filter and process information from our Divine source. As we assimilate information we become a vessel of wisdom that we can teach to others to help them spiritually evolve.

Pisces is the last astrological sign and represents our ability to overcome duality and merge with our higher self. It relates to the musical note B and is located at the crown of the head. This chakra is where we connect with our higher-self. It is the stage of complete enlightenment, open-mindedness and oneness within both the physical and spiritual world. Some of the issues associated with a blocked seventh chakra are the inability to cope with life, anger, rage, fear, anxiety, lack of understanding, fearful of connecting with divinity, and un-open to enlightenment.

In astrology there are three key components to each of our charts – the sun sign, the moon sign, and the ascendant sign. When we play notes that relate to these three signs, the harmony creates balance within our body. Our cells relate to the vibration of the notes. It is very fascinating and I look forward to exploring this in a future book.

Typically, we begin the astrological year with Aries. However, in some years the full moon takes place prior to the new moon. There can be a range of dates for the new and full moons. You can view a schedule of the current year new and full moons at www.NewMoonManifesting.com/moon-phases. The new moon is time to begin anew – start new projects, set new intentions, and relationships.

You can also register at NewMoonManifesting.com for our monthly live conference call around the time of the new moon. It's a great way to stay on track with your goals each month and learn how to work with the characteristics of each astrological sign.

Aries New Moon

March or April

Aries asks, "Who am I?"

<u>Aries Keywords</u>
Action * Reinvent * Authentic * Energetic * Passion * Initiate * Independent * Boldness * Assertive * Survival Instincts * Adventure * Desire * Self-discovery * Leadership * Strength * Instincts * Optimism * Generous * Courageous * Enthusiastic *

Element: Fire - cardinal
Chakra: Root Chakra – First Chakra
Essential Oil Recommendations:
- Lime
- Ginger
- Clove & Melaleuca
- Frankincense, Myrrh, Vetiver & White Fir
- Juniper Berry
- Ylang Ylang

Happy new year – happy new you! Some of you may be wondering what in the world I'm talking about. This isn't the New Year; that happens in January. Although we begin a new calendar year in January, it occurs in the depth of winter. In Chinese medicine, winter is a time of hibernation. It is an introspective time of self-evaluation and integrating what we have resolved over the past year. It's no wonder setting New Year's resolutions often fail. It's time to evaluate and ponder versus initiating something new.

During the nineteen eighties and mid-nineties I was an athletic instructor. I saw the same thing happen every January. People would set great intentions to exercise and get into shape. Yet, within the first 3 weeks half of the new people would drop out, and within 6 weeks my class was back to the regular crowd. Setting our New Year's resolutions and goals is better suited with the Astrological New Year because we are synchronizing our efforts with nature's rhythms. We want to be successful, right? Why not work with the rhythms of nature?

There are patterns to the astrological signs that assist us in our physical and spiritual evolution. Often times we can't achieve our goals in a single lunar cycle. Sometimes they take several cycles, even years to achieve. By tracking your growth with the lunar cycles each year, you have a frame of reference. We can see the changes through the years. Einstein said insanity is doing the same thing over and over again, expecting different results. When we want something to change in our life, we have to change.

When we begin a New Year, we have the opportunity to integrate what we have learned and healed over the previous year. We now operate from a different perspective. These gradual steps move us closer to manifesting all of our goals. As we move through each year, we learn how to stand more firmly in our power, and understand ourselves better.

The Aries New Moon is the beginning of a new astrological year. It is the first of the zodiac signs. It is truly a time of new beginnings. In the northern hemisphere, Aries occurs in the spring. We can take cues from nature as flowers and trees are popping open with blossoms and leaves, and seeds are being planted by farmers for the growing period. There is a sense of renewal and rebirth.

Aries helps us discover *who am I?* Each New Year there is an opportunity to reinvent ourselves. We can use the personal growth and lessons we've learned over the prior twelve astrological signs to start the New Year from a new level.

Aries is a fire sign. Fire signs inspire us to move. They encourage us to take action by igniting our passions. We feel more energetic, assertive, and bold. Have you ever tried to manifest a goal without feeling passion for it? It's impossible! We have to have passion to fuel us, and that's exactly what Aries does. It fuels our fire.

Aries also enhances our survival skills. It helps us figure out how to feel safe and secure in the world. As children we have all experienced some sort of emotional wounds that may cause us to feel insecure and question our ability to survive. This fear skews our thoughts and beliefs causing us to change our behavior and personality. Our ego will do whatever it necessary to sustain our survival. But sometimes our survival isn't threatened, but because our "lens is out of focus," we can't see our behavior and our perspectives may be inaccurate, so we make poor choices.

For example, Jenny is a great attorney. She did well in school but after graduation it took her over a year to get a job in her field. She had to borrow money from her parents, which caused her to feel guilty and ashamed – unable to take care of herself. After three years of working, she hates her job, her boss, and the work she is doing. It's not at all what she imagined. She wants to find another job, yet her ego reminds her, "Remember how difficult it was to get this job? Maybe you should just suck it up and be grateful for it." Sound familiar? We all have those little voices in our head that keep us from taking action; reminding us that we can't do something or dredges up the past. With these unresolved emotions, it's difficult for Jenny to move forward. She will actually attract a similar situation to her until she resolves the emotions and fears.

The past isn't our future. We have experiences to remind us that we have emotions to heal. We consistently project unresolved emotions and concern that we may experience similar emotions or situations from the past. This is the "cause and effect" pattern that keeps us stuck. To overcome her fears, Jenny needs to address the emotions she felt during her transition from law school and similar emotions she felt during her lifetime. We are magnetic beings. We need to shift the internal vibration so we attract a different external circumstance. Sounds easy, right?

Aries helps in doing that. It helps us reset our instincts related to survival. We want to overcome the emotional wounds we have experienced so we can align ourselves abundance versus scarcity.

The New Year is a clean slate making this new moon especially potent. Like all fire signs, the Aries new moon is about taking action. It ignites the passion within and helps us turn desires into results.

Taking action can we overwhelming. We often want to know the entire process, every possible obstacle, or the outcome prior to taking the first step. But that's impossible.

Manifesting is meant to be a co-creative process between us and our higher-self. Our job is to take the steps in front of us, while our higher-self guides us towards the destination. We must have faith or be willing to take steps without knowing the final outcome for the manifesting process to properly work. This means relinquishing control and surrendering to the process.

When we can break down the process of big goals and take small steps towards them, over time we eventually achieve them. We need to let go of perceptions of instant success or gratification and realize this is a process through which there will be personal growth.

Aries relates to the 1st House – the House of Self. This house is centered on new beginnings, the individual, and the voyage of discovery that defines us. It also rules early childhood, and our views of the world are shaped here. It addresses our personality, essential qualities, approach to life, and basic sensibilities. The inner self and outer body are the emphasis of the 1st House. For a more personalized approach, get a copy of your birth chart and see what House falls within Aries for you. Refer to page 164 for additional characteristics of the Astrological Houses since Aries does not fall in the 1st House for all of us. Each month new moon goals can be customized by reviewing your personal birth chart and determining what House the moon falls in at that time.

Aries rules the 1st chakra – the Root Chakra. This is located at the base of the torso and is responsible for helping us learn how to survive.

It includes interaction with our tribe and family to teach us how to be in the world to ensure our survival and security. The first chakra is our connection to the earth. The grounding influence of Mother Earth supports our physical survival by providing the elements we need.

The first chakra is where we learn about the tribal consciousness and collective will power. We absorb the strengths, weaknesses, beliefs, superstitions and fears of the group. Through our interactions with family and groups we learn the power of common beliefs with others. We learn the power of sharing a moral and ethical code handed down over generations.

We are taught to make choices consistent with the group. At some point in our lives we make choices that may go against the beliefs of the family or tribe. This is the first conflict we experience. Evaluating our beliefs is a spiritual and biological necessity for our bodies, minds, and spirits. We require new ideas in order to thrive, grow, and evolve.

Imbalances in the 1st chakra may show up in our system as a lack of energy, vitality, nutritional deficiency, anger, depression, adrenal fatigue, compromised immune system, lower spine issues, elimination organs – kidneys, skin, and colon. It also relates to hip joint issues, bones, muscles, and the blood.

The primary emotion associated with the root chakra is *fear*.

Aries New Moon Questions to Ponder:
What do I like?
What do I want to change?
When do I feel safe and secure in the world?
What fears about survival do I still hold onto?
How do I find balance between independence/dependence?
How can I strengthen my self-esteem?
How do I feel empowered in my life?

Aries New Moon Intentions
For example: I am so grateful that I easily take the action steps necessary to achieve my goals.

Act "as if" dialogue of your intentions:

For example: Allison just called me to share the great news that my book has reached the NY Times best seller list! I'm ecstatic that I took the steps necessary to complete this project. Hearing how people's lives have changed as a result of this book is so thrilling!

_____
_____
_____
_____
_____
_____
_____
_____
_____

Create an empowering question or mantra:

Empowering Question Example: Why is it so easy for me to stand in my power, expressing my individuality while contributing to the collective?

Mantra – Each month come up with a simple mantra or affirmation that helps keep you focused on your New Moon intentions. Mantra example: I am independent, assertive, and easily take action.

_____
_____
_____
_____
_____
_____
_____
_____

Libra Full Moon

March or April

THE LIBRA – ARIES AXIS is the focus for this Full Moon. With every full moon it's important to find balance between the opposing energies. We can only know our self (Aries) when we relate to someone else (Libra).

This full moon highlights imbalances in relationships. Libra emphasizes creating healthy relationships. Healthy relationships are based on compromise, setting boundaries, and standing in our power. This not only includes relationships with other people, but how we relate to everything around us.

We are in relationships with everything – including nature, other people, our health, money, food, addictions, etc. It's important to identify why we are behaving a certain way and how that is influencing our desired results. Relationships are the magnifying glass through which we see ourselves. They reflect back to us parts of ourselves that need to be healed.

When we feel unworthy to receive we end up sabotaging our results. With this full moon look at how everything relates back to you and how certain behaviors are creating current results. The Libra full moon illuminates any areas of codependence, inability to stand up for ourselves, selfish behavior, and emotional conflicts that need to be resolved.

During the full moon, notice what relationships are highlighted or brought to light, typically through conflict or an inability to express personal desires. These are the emotional issues that are cropping up to be explored. As emotions arise, identify exactly what is being felt. As we acknowledge them, we want to release the old and replace it with what we do want. Creating a ritual around releasing unwanted emotions, beliefs, or behavior is helpful. Here are a couple of suggestions:

1) Write down emotions, situations, beliefs, and people you wish to release, then burn the list (in a safe manner) allowing the smoke to carry the old away.
2) Use breath work using the inhale as a cleansing breath, and the exhale to release the old.
3) Use essential oils such as geranium, white fir, and ylang ylang just above the heart. I personally love this combination to release issues related to trust, resolve ancestral patterns stuck in the DNA, and restore optimism to the heart. Feel free to use other essential oils you feel drawn to use. Your body knows what it needs. Also refer to the Libra or Aries New Moon chapters for additional essential oil suggestions.

Whenever we release something, we want to replace or reclaim what we want. For example, if I'm releasing feeling unworthy I want to reclaim abundance and allow myself to receive.

The time between the full moon and the next new moon is a perfect time to go through the release and replace process.

This is a purification process. This is basically being conscious of our thoughts, emotions, behavior, and beliefs so we make sure they are aligned with Universal truth. When we consistently release inaccurate information, we allow wholeness and the pure Divine essence of our soul to be revealed.

Purification takes place on a physical, mental, emotional, and spiritual level. It represents the means through which each soul can recognize and return to the divinity that lies within us.

Find balance with the Libra full moon by honoring the emotions that arise and following your passions. Find ways to be balanced in your relationships while still honoring yourself by setting healthy boundaries and standing in your power. Be expressive and learn how to communicate your desires to feel empowered.

Libra Full Moon Questions to Ponder:

What is being reflected in my relationships right now?
How do I find balance between meeting my needs and what others want?
Who am I partnering with?
Why am I partnering with them at this time?
How do I cooperate and form relationships with others?
Who am I?
How do I rebalance the scales?

Full Moon Release & Reclaim
I release:

_____
_____
_____

I reclaim:

Taurus New Moon

April or May

Taurus asks, "What do I value?"

<u>Taurus Keywords</u>
Dependable * Persistent * Loyal * Patient * Generous * Values Love * Pleasure * Luxury * Beauty * Art * Material comforts * Building * Relationships * Dependable * Culture * Nature * Gratitude * Thoroughness * Foundation * Self-acceptance * Maintaining Structure * Money * Healthy Body Image

Element: Earth - fixed
Chakra: 2nd Chakra – Sexual Chakra
Essential Oil Recommendations:
- Bergamot
- Cinnamon
- Clove
- Clove
- Grapefruit
- Patchouli

TAURUS IS AN EARTH ELEMENT and helps us connect with the senses and pleasures such as touch, taste, and smell. Earth elements help us get in touch with our bodies and feel life through our five senses. Our senses provide revelation of artful things and beauty. Earth signs help us make our dreams real by providing the traction needed to build our lives.

The Taurus new moon helps us determine, "What do I value?" It emphasizes the beauty and love of the physical world such as art, money, pleasure, and luxury. Taurus supports our desires for living an abundant life. This includes an abundance of self-love and self-worth, good friends, good food, and enjoying the physical pleasures of life.

We cultivate abundance through self-sufficiency, disciplined effort, utilizing available resources, being thorough, building a foundation, creating material comforts, and persistently working towards our goals.

The new moon holds promise for transforming the way we think, communicate, and what we value most. This new moon emphasizes and helps us transform whatever we value.

Taurus rules the 2nd House – The House of Value. Here we are immersed in the material and immaterial things of certain value. This includes our belongings, money, acquisitions, property, as well as our growth and self-worth. Refer to page xx164 for additional characteristics of the Astrological Houses.

Taurus relates to the sexual chakra located just below the 2nd chakra in the lower abdomen area. Taurus wants us to learn what we value in life, how we value life, what sustains us, what motivates us or how we view our power, strength, and safety in the world.

Our sexual impulses are a powerful driving force. They may be used inappropriately to manipulate or control others in order to get what we want. When we learn what motivates us we can use it to expand our creativity.

Imbalances in this chakra can be seen in bladder, kidney, and issues in the large intestine. Also issues related to the pelvic area, sex organs – testicles and ovaries.

The primary fear associated with this chakra is the fear of pleasure, and guilt associated with pleasure.

Taurus New Moon Questions to Ponder:
What do I value above all else right now?
What makes me feel valued?
What can I give myself to feel more comfortable?
How can I express myself through art, entertaining, other pleasure?
How can I spend more time in nature?
When can I schedule an aromatherapy massage?

Taurus New Moon Intentions
For example: I am so grateful that I spend time with my family and friends, entertaining and traveling. I easily enjoy the comforts of life.

_____

_____

_____

_____

_____

_____

_____

_____

Act "as if" dialogue of your intentions:

For example: One of my favorite bands came to town and the concert immediately sold out. A radio station was giving away tickets and I won them! We got front row tickets and the best part – we got to meet the band and hang out with them after the show. It ended up being more of a philosophical discussion and music and inspiration. We had such an amazing time! I love enjoying the pleasures of life!

Create an empowering question or mantra:

Empowering Question Example: Why is it so easy for me to fully enjoy life?

Mantra Example: I enjoy life fully and bask in the fruits of my success!

Scorpio Full Moon

April or May

THE SCORPIO – TAURUS AXIS reminds us to find balance between what we value (Taurus) and what we need to transform (Scorpio) to get there.

The full moon energy is raw and uninhibited. It relates to external situations which show up in blaming outside circumstances or people for situations in our lives. There is a tendency to project our own state of restlessness onto other people. Being aware of this helps us consciously manage emotions and reactions.

The Scorpio full moon takes us deep into illusions and stories we tell ourselves that keep us from achieving our goals. Scorpio wants to purge and release pent up energy and emotions. At times it appears to be easier to hold onto the old story or blame other people for our results. But Scorpio assists us in restructuring the areas of our lives that haven't been working.

It pushes us out of our comfort zone, causing us to address painful memories, addictions, or emotional wounds. Scorpio wants us to resolve these and reinvent a healthier, happier version of ourselves. The water signs are always a deeply emotional time. They help us clean out the old, making room for better situations, things, and relationships.

Opposite of the Scorpio moon we have the Taurus sun. The Taurus sun prefers to skim the surface, and look at the superficial versus facing the emotional stuff. It wants to eat, drink, and be merry; enjoying the finer things in life. It focuses on that which is mine – including personal values, possessions, security, and material goods.

The goal with any full moon is to find balance between these two opposing influences. The Scorpio full moon is not an easy energy to work with. It forces us to dig deep into transforming the past. As we let go and flow with the process, we allow space for new opportunities and growth.

During the full moon, take note of outward relationships. These are a reflection of inner emotions and patterns that need to be resolved. For example, wishing someone else would change is a reflection and reminder that this is probably something within us that needs to be resolved.

As emotions arise, we want to acknowledge and release them. Creating a ritual around releasing them is a helpful tool. Here are a couple of suggestions:

1) Write down emotions, situations, beliefs, and people you wish to release, then burn the list (in a safe manner) allowing the smoke to carry the old away.
2) Use breath work utilizing the inhale as a cleansing breath, and the exhale to release the old.
3) Use essential oils such as lavender (calming), frankincense (seeing the truth) and/or sandalwood just below the throat or along the spine to support balancing, standing in our truth and following our divine

purpose. Feel free to use other essential oils you are drawn towards. Your body knows what it needs. Also, refer to the Scorpio or Taurus New Moon chapters for additional essential oil suggestions.

Whenever we release something it's best to replace it with what we want. The time between the full moon and the next new moon is a perfect time to go through the release and replace process. This is the purification process. When we our conscious of our thoughts, emotions, behavior, and beliefs, we can change incorrect ones to align with universal truth. When we consistently release inaccurate information, we allow wholeness and the pure Divine essence of our soul to be revealed.

Purification takes place on a physical, mental, emotional, and spiritual level. It represents the means through which each soul can recognize and return to the divinity that lies within.

Find balance with the Scorpio full moon by honoring the emotions that arise and embrace your passions. Allow your passions to follow your soul's deepest desires. Ultimately passion is the basis of power and supports us in creating the life we want.

Scorpio Full Moon Questions to Ponder:
How do I overcome the shadow aspects of myself?
What do I feel passion about?
What do I need to transform?
What is my relationship with the life force flowing through me?
What new ways do I desire to use my creative life force to manifest my passion?
What do I need to change in my life to create greater intimacy with others?

Full Moon Release & Reclaim

I release:

I reclaim:

Gemini New Moon

May or June

Gemini asks, "What do I think?"

<u>Gemini Basic Tools</u>
Imaginative * Communicating * Intelligence * Writing * Speaking * Logic * Social * Networking * Listening * Clever * Curious * Expressive * Quick Thinking * Energetic * Adaptable Power of Language * Ingenuity * Social Ease * Information

Element: Air - mutable
Chakra: 2nd Chakra (sacral) – creative fire
Essential Oil Recommendations:
- Lavender
- Wild Orange
- Cedarwood
- Cilantro
- Bergamot
- Cinnamon
- Cassia

WITH THE GEMINI NEW MOON, it's a good time to be open, interested, curious, and communicate ideas with other people. Gemini brings in mental energies and focuses on the conscious mind. It provides the foundation for speaking, writing, and teaching. There may be expansion around new ideas with the Gemini cycle, so think outside the box. It's also a good time to be open to inspiration and ideas that lead us closer to our goals. Be mindful of new information, conveying ideas, expanding learning, and asking questions without becoming overly analytical. There may be unique messages that help take goals to a new level.

Gemini is a very social sign. It's a good time to join a group and network where ideas can be communicated. It is a highly active sign where multi-tasking may be effortless. It also is a great time to write letters, emails, and read materials.

Gemini represents duality in our lives. It is symbolized as the twins. It helps us see all sides of the question and multiple solutions. It's a good time to listen to our inner wisdom as well as applying rational thought.

Gemini rules the 3rd House – the House of Communication. This is a good time to re-evaluate communication skills. Sometimes being a good communicator means we need to listen more. It's important to listen to the viewpoints of others without defending our position. There may be surprising clues that provides needed guidance. It's also a good time to improve skills through education, expand intelligence, heal issues related to childhood wounds, and focus on achievements. Refer to page xx164 for additional characteristics of the Astrological Houses.

Since Gemini is such a strong, mental energy, make sure to protect the nervous system through meditation, yoga, exercise, spending time in nature, and using essential oils. These tools will help release excess mental energy and calm the body.

Gemini is associated with the 2nd chakra – the sacral chakra, located just below the navel. This chakra is responsible for helping us communicate our ideas to the creative center, the Solar Plexus. This is our center of gestation. Gestation includes not only physical procreation, but also the creation of ideas.

The 2nd chakra relates to our beliefs around money, power, and sex as well as how balanced we are in personal relationships. It affects the reproductive organs, large intestine, lower vertebrae, pelvis, appendix, bladder, and hips.

Imbalances in this chakra are reflected in lower back pain, circulation issues, infertility issues, sexual organ issues, painful or frequent urination, edema, leg pain, and addictions. The primary fear related to this chakra is the fear of change and fear of pleasure.

Gemini New Moon Questions to Ponder:
How can I communicate more effectively?
How do I speak my truth?
How can I expand my social circle?
What makes me happy?
What skills can I enhance or new training can I take?
Where can I increase my mindfulness and alertness?
How do I develop deeper relationships with others?
What new course or class do I want to take?

Gemini New Moon Intentions

For example: I easily communicate and express my ideas.

_____

_____

_____

_____   _____

_____

_____

_____

_____

Act "as if" dialogue of your intentions:

For example: I had to call my friend Jaimie today to share my amazing day. I was the key note speaker at a conference for holistic healers. I shared information about business development and taught them how to make more money and serve more people. Many of the participants came up to me afterwards and thanked me for the invaluable information. They are all so excited to implement it in their businesses. I love seeing the light go on when people have ah-ha moments and get it. I'm so grateful for this opportunity.

_____

_____

_____

_____

_____

_____

Create an empowering question or mantra:

Empowering Question Example: Why is it so easy for me to expand my ideas and bring them to fruition?

Mantra Example: I love and accept myself exactly the way I am now.

Sagittarius Full Moon

May or June

THE SAGITTARIUS – GEMINI AXIS reminds us to find balance between looking at envisioning our higher purpose (Sagittarius) and being logical and rational (Gemini).

Sagittarius is fun, fiery, and expansive; pushing us to shoot for the stars and swing big. Sagittarius helps us connect with our soul-self seeking answers to big questions such as, "Why am I here?" "What is my purpose?"

Sagittarius reminds us to listen to our intuitive side, and learn to trust our gut instincts. During this full moon, there may be inspiration that shifts gears or opens new channels towards achieving your new moon intentions.

With every full moon there is a natural tendency to feel that we are being pulled in two directions. This month the conflict arises between logic (Gemini) and faith (Sagittarius). The lesson is to find balance between the two. If we are too analytical then we miss important clues. When we live only by faith, we miss the human aspect of our experience here.

During this full moon take note of spontaneous ideas, inspiration, or that twinge of excitement. There may be opportunities to take big leaps. Sagittarius helps us break through conditioning and soar with a higher vision. With this full moon entertain possibilities that provide a zing of optimism or cause us to flutter with excitement.

Sometimes the Sagittarius energy is so inspiring and exciting that we over-commit our resources. We are committing to our highest spiritual perspective with Sagittarius. Be excited about the momentum, but leave room for everything to come together in the right timeframe.

During the full moon, be open to following life's unpredictable ups and downs from a new or more enlightened perspective. Emotions are heightened with the full moon. We want to acknowledge and release whatever is coming up. Creating a ritual around releasing them is helpful in the healing process. Here are a couple of suggestions:

1) Write down emotions, situations, beliefs, and people you wish to release, then burn the list (in a safe manner) allowing the smoke to carry the old away.
2) Use breath work using the inhale as a cleansing breath, and the exhale to release the old.
3) Use essential oils such as lavender, frankincense, geranium, Roman Chamomile, black pepper, or cedarwood at the base of the skull or along the spine. Feel free to use other essential oils you feel drawn to use. Your body knows what it needs. Also, refer to the Sagittarius or Gemini New Moon chapters for additional essential oil suggestions.

Whenever we release something it's best to replace it with what we want. The time between the full moon and the next new moon is a perfect time to go through the release and replacement process. We are purifying by being aware of our thoughts, emotions, behavior, and beliefs so we make sure they are rooted in universal truth. When we consistently release inaccurate information, we allow wholeness and the pure Divine essence of our soul to be revealed.

Purification takes place on a physical, mental, emotional, and spiritual level. It represents the means through which each soul can recognize and return to the divinity that lies within.

Find balance with the Sagittarius full moon by honoring the emotions that arise and following your passions. Sagittarius reminds us that we are on a voyage of discovery. Along the way we face lessons, our ideals, and the unknown that shape our ethics and beliefs. Find ways to allow your passions to follow the soul's desires. Ultimately passion is the basis of power and supports us in creating the life we desire.

Sagittarius Full Moon Questions to Ponder:
How satisfied am I with my connection to family and community?
How can I trust my higher self more?
Do I share from a truthful, enlightened place with people close to me?
How do I enhance my spiritual connection?
Do I approach life from a place of passion and excitement or security and comfort?
Am I satisfied with my results?
How attentive am I to the physical needs of my body?
What needs to change to allow more self-care time?
How can I have more fun in life?

Full Moon Release & Reclaim

I release:

I reclaim:

Cancer New Moon

June or July

Cancer asks, "What do I feel?"

<u>Cancer Keywords</u>
Emotional * Domestic * Sympathy * Sensitiveness * Artistry
Understanding * Tenacity * Protectiveness * Caring * Nurturing
Maternal * Empathy * Intimacy * Needs * Inner focus * Moods
Home * Family * Environment * Nourishment * Growth

Element: Water - cardinal
Chakra: Between 2nd & 3rd Chakra - Duality
Essential Oil Recommendations:
- Myrrh
- Geranium
- Lemongrass
- Black Pepper
- Clove
- Ginger
- Ylang Ylang

CANCER IS A CARDINAL WATER SIGN. Cardinal signs represent beginnings and initiations. It is the first new moon of the summer. As such, Cancer is assertive, a self-starter, and a go-getter. Since it is a water sign, Cancer is intuitive, feeling, and nurturing. Cancer is led by emotions and is focused on building a family and acquiring domestic security.

This Cancer new moon reveals the power of our emotions. Emotions set the stage for what we love and value. They enhance or block intuition, creativity, and imagination. This is a good moon to focus on setting up the comforts of home, nurturing relationships, and following passions.

Cancer, being a water sign, supports our emotional side. It reminds us to nurture ourselves as well as others. Cancer is the archetype of the Mother – compassionate and caring. She reminds us that as we learn to overcome obstacles we learn compassion. With compassion we expand our ability to love ourselves and others deeply. Our perceptions shift and we see the world differently.

Cancer intensifies our emotions. We pick up the mood of the room with its empathetic qualities. We are all affected by other people's emotions. This lunar cycle would be a good one to practice identifying what emotions belong to others and which are our own. For some reason, we feel it is necessary to carry other people's emotional baggage, which weighs us down.

The Cancer energy is a reminder to stop this, and let other people be responsible for their own emotions and to fight their own battles. Release the need to find solutions for everyone (mother). We take power away from others by doing this. A good mother knows she will not always be there to take care of the child. She must provide her child with skills to manage their emotions, make decisions, and be responsible for their life.

Cancer rules the 4th House – the House of Home & Family. Take time to focus on personal development, honoring what develops a sense of security. This is a time to listen to our gut instincts and honor them. Exploring and developing inner security is supported with Cancer. It's a good time to re-organize and be aware of our roots – especially related to intimacy and vulnerability. It's a good time to create a support system (family) with those who help us feel comfortable. Refer to page 164 for additional characteristics of the Astrological Houses.

The chakra associated with Cancer is located between the 2nd and 3rd chakras. It represents our dual nature and learning to manifest in human form what we desire on a higher plane.

This chakra supports the power center – the Solar Plexus. It is associated with our emotional intelligence and affects our self-confidence. When balanced, we are confident, playful, have the ability to meet challenges, and maintain inner harmony.

Imbalances in this chakra may show up in the form of a person being emotionally cold, having poor discipline, and blaming others. There may be physical issues such as digestion problems, liver issues, autonomic nervous issues, gall bladder and spleen issues, and lower back issues.

The primary fear here is loss of power and inability to act as an individual.

Cancer New Moon Questions to Ponder:
How do I nurture, nourish, and care for myself?
How can I be more sensitive and caring for others?
What can I do to make my home feel more comfortable?
What emotional needs should I address now?
How do I express my artistry?
How do I enhance my environment?

Cancer New Moon Intentions
For example: I am so grateful that I easily nurture myself and others.

_____

_____

_____

_____

_____

_____

_____

Act "as if" dialogue of your intentions:

For example: I had to call my friend Jaimie today to share my amazing day. I was the key note speaker at a conference for holistic healers. I shared information about business development and taught them how to make more money and serve more people. Many of the participants came up to me afterwards and thanked me for the invaluable information. They are all so excited to implement it in their practices. I love seeing the light go on when people have ah-ha moments and get it. I'm so grateful for this opportunity

_____

_____

_____

_____

_____

_____

Create an empowering question or mantra:

Empowering Question Example: Why is it so easy for me to identify what I feel and manage my emotions?

Mantra Example: I am nurturing, compassionate, and mindful of my feelings.

Capricorn Full Moon

June or July

THE CAPRICORN – CANCER AXIS reminds us to seek balance between worldly success (Capricorn) and nurturing our inner world (Cancer). Ignoring either axis may be unhealthy.

The Capricorn full moon reminds us to focus on our success in the world, duty, and obligation. It reflects any imbalances such as working too much or too little, or reveals cracks in our foundational beliefs.

Capricorn encourages us to be grown up and responsible. It influences career, independence, finances, and how we make money. It is the archetype of the Father. Think of it as the part of us that takes care of our outer needs.

The Cancer sun is the archetype of the mother. It is nurturing and influences our home base, our roots, origin, and dependence on others. This is the mother caring for the inner needs. This polarity reminds us to find balance between career and family life.

The Cancer sun shows up in our emotions. Emotions are our guidance system. They are an indicator of how we really feel about situations, ourselves, and other people. When feelings are suppressed or discounted, it comes out in other areas. Look at any time where emotions have been suppressed or avoided. Emotional avoidance may show up in addictive behaviors such as shopping, food, exercise, alcohol, and any other substance or behavior that serves as an escape from emotions.

During the full moon, take note of emotions and situations that create agitated feelings. As emotions arise, we want to acknowledge and release them. Creating a ritual around releasing them is a helpful tool. Here are a couple of suggestions:

1) Write down emotions, situations, beliefs, and people you wish to release, then burn the list (in a safe manner) allowing the smoke to carry the old away.
2) Use breath work using the inhale as a cleansing breath, and the exhale to release the old.
3) Use essential oils such as frankincense, sandalwood, lavender, or Clary Sage over the Third Eye or along the spine. Using fennel or coriander to support increasing or improving the ability to be responsible. Feel free to use other essential oils you feel drawn to use. Your body knows what it needs. Also refer to the Capricorn or Cancer New Moon chapters for additional essential oil suggestions.

Whenever we release something it's best to replace it with what we want. The time between the full moon and the next new moon is a perfect time to go through the release and replace process. This is a purification process. Which means we are aware of our thoughts, emotions, behavior, and beliefs, so we make sure they are aligned with universal truth. When we consistently release inaccurate information, we allow wholeness and the pure Divine essence of our soul to be revealed.

Purification takes place on a physical, mental, emotional, and spiritual level. It represents the means through which each soul can recognize and return to the divinity that lies within.

Find balance with the Capricorn full moon by honoring the emotions that arise and following your passions. Find ways to allow your passions to align with your soul's desires. Ultimately passion is the basis of power and supports us in creating the life we desire.

Capricorn also reminds us of our responsibility for our thoughts, emotions, beliefs, behavior, and understanding how all of this connects to our physical reality. These fundamental elements are vital in manifesting more.

Capricorn Full Moon Questions to Ponder:
How do I find balance between caring for myself and others?
What do I feel passion about?
How do I create security for myself?
Where am I co-dependent?
How can I trust in the Divine to support ALL of my needs?
How can my passion become my contribution to society?
How do I stand in my power and create the life I crave?
How do I follow my soul's desires?
How can I balance being responsible with self-care?
How do I care for myself?
Do I honor and value my feelings?

Full Moon Release & Reclaim

I release:

I reclaim:

Leo New Moon

July or August

Leo asks, "What do I Love?"

<u>Leo Keywords</u>
Kindness * Confident * Extrovert * Spontaneous * Ambitious * Generous * Loyal * Fun * Encouraging * Enthusiasm * Creative Expressive * Risk Taking * Dramatic * Determined * Noble * Independent * Zest for life * Dignity * Leadership * Radiant * Vitality * Authority * Affection * Children * Child-like * Will *

Element: Fire - Fixed
Chakra: 3rd Chakra Solar Plexus
Essential Oil Recommendations:
- Wild Orange
- Ylang Ylang
- Oregano
- Grapefruit
- Rosemary
- Clove & Ginger

LEO IS A FIXED FIRE SIGN. It is forceful, magnetic, generous, and impulsive. It would rather move through the heart than through reason. Like the lion, Leo is commanding, courageous, high-spirited, and assertive. This energy supports us in standing in our power and following our heart's desires. How can we be more noble, and unconcerned about what others think of us? There is no need to prove ourselves to anyone. The Leo new moon reminds us to expand our creative self-expression and follow our heart.

Leo rules the 5th House – the House of Family. It reminds us to concentrate on our family, relationships, and communicating on a personal level. It also addresses creation of art and culture. The creative life helps us determine what we like and dislike; what brings us pleasure versus pain. Emotional satisfaction is affected by this House. There is a willingness to take risks related to love, money, and life in hopes of a pleasurable outcome. Refer to page 164 for additional characteristics of the Astrological Houses.

Leo relates to our 3rd chakra – the Solar Plexus. This is the energy center of personal power. It supports our creative impulses. It teaches us to stand in our power, claiming our authentic power, and reminding us to follow our passion. It's a good cycle to let go of other people's opinions or how society tells us we should be. It encourages us to listen to our gut instinct and inner promptings of what makes us happy and feel successful.

This is our personal power center. It is the energy center of action, willpower, self-confidence, self-respect, self-esteem, and a sense of responsibility. It is located about two inches above the navel. The Solar Plexus is the energy center responsible for digesting life. It influences the stomach, spleen, kidneys, liver, pancreas, lower esophagus, and middle spine.

The primary emotion associated with the Solar Plexus is anger. Anger is usually a reaction related to one feeling unable to manage their power or feel powerful. Perhaps there are emotions such as feeling embarrassed, frustrated, inadequate, or incapable. This can be seen in the angry teenager learning how to interact in the world. Without experiences the teen makes poor choices. They often feel powerless because other people are controlling their choices and restricting their power.

When there is an imbalance in power, it affects our ability to believe we deserve to receive. We may feel unworthy to receive and have self-worth issues. As a result of the power imbalances, behavior such as defensiveness, competitiveness, being aggressive, passive-aggressive or slipping into addictions may occur.

Imbalances in the Solar Plexus may show up as digestive issues, ulcers, acid reflux, heartburn, diabetes, and eating disorders. Also, signs of an underactive Solar Plexus typically show up as feelings of powerlessness and low self-esteem. Signs of an overactive Solar Plexus may show up as excessive anger, fear, hatred, or the need to control or dominate others to feel superior or powerful.

When fully balanced, its primary strengths include a healthy self-esteem, self-respect, self-discipline, ambition, the ability to generate action, and handle crisis. There is also the courage to take risks, be generous, have ethics, and express strength of character.

The spiritual goal of this chakra is to help us mature in our self-understanding, the relationship we have with ourselves, to stand on our own, and take care of ourselves.

Self-understanding and acceptance, the bond we form with ourselves, is in many ways the most crucial spiritual challenge we face. In truth, if we cannot like ourselves, we will be incapable of making healthy decisions. Instead we direct all personal power for decision making into the hands of someone else; someone we want to impress, someone we think has authority over us, or someone we believe will provide physical security.

The Solar Plexus is sometimes called the gut instinct. It is the seat of our knowingness as to whether something feels right to us or feels that power is being taken away. As we develop a healthy sense of self, we trust our intuitive voice and follow our inner guidance and gut instincts.

The primary fear with this chakra is the ability to act and be an individual. Shame is the primary emotion associated with it.

With this new moon think about expansion; like all fire signs it gives us a dose of courage to take bigger risks than may feel comfortable. This is a good moon to set and enforce better boundaries, learn to stand in your power, express yourself, and effectively communicate your likes and dislikes; by doing so we gain self-respect, confidence, and the respect of others.

Leo New Moon Questions to Ponder:
What creative juices are sparked with the Leo moon?
How can I have more fun?
Where can I express love more freely?
Where can I find more pleasure in life?
How can I be more childlike and curious?
How can I be more courageous and take action?

Leo New Moon Intentions

For example: I find fun in all aspects of life. I easily stand in my power. I take calculated risks towards my goals.

_____

_____

_____

_____

_____

_____

Act "as if" dialogue of your intentions:

For example: It feels so good to follow my heart's desires and passion to assist other people in learning how to create what they want through classes, speaking, books, and programs I offer. My work no longer feels like work – it is joyful and I feel at peace in all I do. The Universe is very generous as I am generous with others.

_____

_____

_____

_____

_____

_____

_____

_____

_____

Create an empowering question or mantra:

Empowering Question Example: Why is it so easy for me to stand in my power? Why is my life so much fun?

Mantra Example: Fun with friends and family keep my life joyous and exciting.

Aquarius Full Moon

July or August

THE AQUARIUS – LEO AXIS is the focus of this full moon. It is a reminder to find balance between how we relate to our authentic self (Leo) and the collective self (Aquarius).

The full moon illuminates what has been hiding in our psyche and brings it to light. These hidden aspects could be things we have overlooked or issues we are unaware of, yet they limit our ability to manifest.

Aquarius is the water-bearer. She pours her knowledge over humanity. The Aquarius full moon reminds us to express our authentic self (Leo) in a way that encourages diversity in our thoughts, science, truth, and freedom. The *"new age"* reflects diversity of thought – by allowing others to have different opinions and honoring them without the need to prove our position. Aquarius dares us to break traditions. It is rebellious. It motivates us to work toward the betterment of everyone as we all become empowered and enlightened.

The focus of healing with the Aquarius full moon relates to resolving issues around false power, releasing the need to take power away from others as well as, setting better boundaries so we stand in our power. When we no longer take power from others, nor allow others to take power from us, we connect more deeply with our authentic self. As a result there are opportunities for healing misperceptions. When we do our part by taking responsibility for our own healing, the collective consciousness benefits. Our healing raises our personal vibration, which also increases the vibration of the planet – helping everyone heal and evolve.

During the full moon, there may be surprising breakthroughs. Aquarius is like an unexpected breeze on a hot summer night. In the midst of struggle there are surprising events that break patterns and shift perceptions. Follow the path that is illuminated as you work though emotional issues that arise. As emotions surface, we want to acknowledge and release them. Creating a ritual around releasing them is a helpful tool. Here are a couple of suggestions:

1) Write down emotions, situations, beliefs, and people you wish to release, then burn the list (in a safe manner) allowing the smoke to carry the old away.
2) Use breath work using the inhale as a cleansing breath and the exhale to release the old.
3) Use essential oils such as Clary sage, lavender, Melissa, Roman Chamomile, over the Third Eye and cedarwood on the bottom of the feet or along the spine. Feel free to use other essential oils you feel drawn to use. Your body knows what it needs. Also refer to the Aquarius or Leo New Moon chapters for additional essential oil suggestions.

Whenever we release something it's best to replace it with what we want. The time between the full moon and the next new moon is a perfect time to go through the release and replace process. This is a purification process. Which means we are aware of our thoughts, emotions, behavior, and beliefs, so we make sure they are aligned with universal truth. When we consistently release inaccurate information, we allow wholeness and the pure Divine essence of our soul to be revealed.

Purification takes place on a physical, mental, emotional, and spiritual level. It represents the means through which each soul can recognize and return to the divinity that lies within.

Find balance with the Aquarius full moon by honoring the emotions that arise and following your passions. Find ways to allow your passions to follow the soul's desires. Ultimately passion is the basis of power and supports us in creating the life we desire.

Use this lunation to expand humanitarian services, independence, and freedom. Expand social connections and create a better world through equality and social justice for all.

Aquarius Full Moon Questions to Ponder:

What does true freedom mean to me?
Am I leading my life from a place of inner authority?
How can my passion become my contribution to society?
What steps am I taking to embrace my inner passions?
How do I follow my soul's desires?
How do I perceive my future?
Am I standing in my power?
Where do power struggles still exist in my life?
How do I support equality for other people?
How can I break through conformity and allow radical new thinking to emerge?
Where is my life taking quantum spiritual leaps this year?

Full Moon Release & Reclaim

I release:

I reclaim:

Virgo New Moon

August or September

Virgo asks, "What do I Purify?"

<u>Virgo Keywords</u>
Stable * Mental Pursuits * Work Activities * Service * Routine * Attention to Details * Analyze * Healthy Habits * Perfection * Exercise * Efficiency * Critical Thinking * Clever * Planning * Strategizing * Discernment * Observant * Reliable * Precise *

Element: Earth - mutable
Chakra: 4th Chakra – Heart (lower)
Essential Oil Recommendations:
- Geranium
- Cypress
- Peppermint
- Lime
- White Fir or Pine
- Eucalyptus
- Lemon

THE VIRGO NEW MOON helps us get back to routines, clear away the clutter, get organized, and clarify existing goals.

Virgo represents the virgin. She is practical, grounded, and analytical. She is a mutable earth sign which means she is flexible, and easily adapts to any situation. This is great advice for all of us in our manifesting journey. Flexibility seems to be a valuable skill versus being stubborn and rigid in our perceptions of how manifesting should transpire.

Capitalize on the Virgo energy by determining where clutter exists physically, emotionally, and mentally. It's a good time to clear it away allowing space for new ideas, inspiration, assistance, and support to fill in the gaps.

Virgo carries with it an air of perfectionism, efficiency, and flexibility. She prepares us for the fall where we harvest the fruits of our labor – primarily the seeds that were planted with the Aries new moon several months ago. She is a dynamic problem solver, developing creative solutions that take us closer to our goals. Skills involving critical analysis are heightened with the Virgo energy. There may be interesting solutions related to furthering our goals during this time. Steer clear of feeling the need to be perfect, striving to do our best is the answer to offset perceptions of perfection.

Evaluating healthy habits, re-establishing routines, and setting intentions around strengthening the mind, body, and spirit are advised. This includes eating better quality food, drinking plenty of water, exercising regularly, meditating daily, going back to school or expanding your skills in other ways. These are all examples of how to use the support of Virgo.

Virgo's themes relate to rituals of daily life – especially related to food and harvesting. Since Virgo is an earth sign, look at how the earth feeds and nourishes us. Also, habits around how we create a sustainable environment and how we care for the vulnerable in our society are issues that will be in focus over the next couple of years.

This is a great new moon to re-commit to getting back on track with what we want to accomplish over the next few months.

Virgo rules the 6th House – the House of Health. This includes the ability to maintain healthy habits while coping with adversity and change. Crises, illnesses and reversals of fortune are all a part of our human experience. How we respond to these situations and deal with the lessons they teach us helps to define the person we become. The 6th House addresses the daily dealings of life. These simple matters keep our engines running and enable us to do more important work of our choosing. Refer to page 164 for additional characteristics of the Astrological Houses.

Virgo relates to the 4th Chakra – the Heart Chakra (lower heart). This relates to our ability to connect to life. It is the seat of compassion and willingness to help, as well as our happiness and sincerity.

Imbalances in the heart chakra show up as chest pain, lung congestion, upper back tension, blood pressure imbalances, circulation imbalances, and immune deficiency. The primary fear is being unloved. Grief is the primary emotion associated with the heart.

Virgo helps us re-commit to ourselves and get back on track by encouraging us to create healthy habits such as creating a new exercise routine, getting a check-up, or eating better. It also is a good time to take on any projects that need critical analysis, problem solving, strategizing, or creating efficiency. Re-organize to make life simpler.

Virgo New Moon Questions to Ponder:

What health habits or routines do I want to change?
How can I take better care of my health?
When can I de-junk my space?
How can I be more organized?
How do I like my job or career?
What skills or training can I do to enhance it?

Virgo New Moon Intentions

For example: I am healthy, happy, and strong, always striving to do my best.

_____

_____

_____

_____

_____

_____

_____

_____

Act "as if" dialogue of your intentions:

For example: I'm so excited to have reached my optimal health goal. I feel amazing! I've been working very hard to create health exercise and eating habits. It was easy to stay on track because I felt so motivated to restore my health. I'm had a team of people encouraging me in the process. And it feels good to have taken these steps for myself.

_____

_____

_____

_____
_____
_____
_____
_____

Create an empowering question or mantra:

Empowering Question Example: Why is it so easy for me to be organized and efficient?

Mantra Example: I am healthy, wealthy, and wise.

_____
_____
_____
_____
_____
_____
_____
_____
_____
_____
_____
_____
_____
_____

Pisces Full Moon

August or September

THE PISCES – VIRGO AXIS reminds us to reflect on how we integrate our spirituality (Pisces) with our ideals (Virgo). The key to success here is maintaining order in our daily lives while expressing our spiritual needs.

Pisces is a mutable water sign and all water signs are a time of turning inward. Expect to be more sensitive, in-tune, emotional, and receptive. The full moon unearths whatever is lurking in our shadow side. It brings up emotional wounds, feeling unsupported, questions about spiritual development, unresolved pain, and addictions. It's a rich time to acknowledge whatever we are faced with and supports us to resolve these situations and emotions.

Pisces helps us dig deep into the body, mind, and heart. As we learn to resolve these hidden emotions, we surrender to the healing process. Pisces highlights how we have been sabotaging ourselves. Any limitations and fears are illuminated as we see how we have been getting in our own way. To overcome fears and limitations ask, "Why do I hold on to particular behaviors, and beliefs?" Awareness is the key to providing clarity into how we contribute to our existing results.

The full moon is a reflection of what is occurring internally. Issues we need to face show up in other people's behavior and habits that annoy or upset us. Instead of judging others, look at their behavior and determine where you are exhibiting the same ones. By looking within we determine where we behave in a similar way. It's often easier to blame other people and point the finger than take responsibility for our own stuff. Shift the focus inward and resolve unwanted behaviors and patterns.

Virgo supports us at this time by encouraging us to work on skills that support abundance on all levels. Structure, routine, healthy habits, and critical thinking are all characteristics of Virgo. Use this energy to shift old habits into healthier ones. Virgo also supports vitality, love, fulfillment, income, and joy. Take time to make self-care a priority by feeding the mind, body, and spirit.

This harvest full moon is emotional, so be flexible and go with the flow. Pisces cleanses our emotional realms. There is potential for deep healing.

During the full moon, acknowledge emotions that are rising up. Be sensitive to an opening of expanded possibilities. Follow the path that is illuminated as you work though emotional issues brought to the surface. As emotions arise, acknowledge and release them. Creating a ritual around releasing them is a helpful tool. Here are a couple of suggestions:

1) Write down emotions, situations, beliefs, and people you wish to release, then burn the list (in a safe manner) allowing the smoke to carry the old away.
2) Use breath work using the inhale as a cleansing breath, and the exhale to release the old.

3) Use essential oils such as Melissa, Roman Chamomile, frankincense, sandalwood, juniper berry, rose or rosemary over the crown of the head or along the spine. Feel free to use other essential oils you feel drawn to use. Your body knows what it needs. Also, refer to the Pisces or Virgo New Moon chapters for additional essential oil suggestions.

Whenever we release something it's best to replace it with what we want. The time between the full moon and the next new moon is a perfect time to go through the release and replace process. This is a purification process, where we are mindful of our thoughts, emotions, behavior, and beliefs, and align them with universal truth. When we consistently release inaccurate information, we allow wholeness and the pure Divine essence of our soul to be revealed.

Purification takes place on a physical, mental, emotional, and spiritual level. It represents the means through which each soul can recognize and return to the divinity that lies within.

Find balance with the Pisces full moon by honoring the emotions that arise and following your passions. Explore ways to allow your passions to align with your soul's desires. Passion is the spice of life that supports us in creating the life we desire.

Pisces Full Moon Questions to Ponder:
How does my vision for world harmony make me stretch beyond my comfort zone?
How do I follow my soul's desires?
How do I attune my desires to serve humanity more?
What delusions do I need to remove?
How can I contribute to creating more harmony, peace and cooperation?

Full Moon Release & Reclaim

I release:

_____
_____
_____
_____
_____
_____
_____
_____
_____
_____

I reclaim:

_____
_____
_____
_____
_____
_____
_____
_____
_____
_____

Libra New Moon

September or October

Libra asks, "How do I relate to others?"

<u>Libra Keywords</u>
Balance * Kind * Gentle * Lovers of Beauty * Harmony * Peace Romantic * Charming * Diplomatic * Graceful * Idealistic * Hospitable * Forward Thinking * Reflective * Sociable * Impartial * Sensitive * Optimism * Justice * Loving * Elegance

Element: Air - Cardinal
Chakra: 4th Chakra Heart – Thymus (high heart)
Essential Oil Recommendations:
- Rose
- Geranium
- Cypress
- Peppermint
- White Fir
- Eucalyptus
- Thyme

LIBRA REMINDS US TO BALANCE all aspects of our lives. It emphasizes love and relationships, and how important it is to balance them, make peace with existing conflicts, improve negotiating skills, and seek love and beauty. It is a cardinal sign and represents a new season – fall.

The Libra new moon is a time of greater clarity since we are balancing the scales. The scales of Libra area a symbolic representation of balance between our self and others. Libra loves relationships, peace, and harmony. This doesn't come from giving in but from meeting the other's point of view with an open heart, understanding, and compassion. Libra wants everyone to win – there is no need to overpower others. As we value other people's opinions and perspectives, we find peace.

Libra may spark a new love interest, create new business partnerships, or breathe life into existing personal and business relationships. It reminds us to be powerful, but not dominating or controlling.

Libra rules the 7th House – The House of Partnerships. In this House we begin to shift our focus from ourselves and include others. By cooperating and relating with others, we unite for the purpose of achieving something. As we unite with others, we enhance our ability to achieve a greater good for our community or collective conscious. Cooperation and partnerships help expedite our life's purpose. Ideas flow and grow as a result of working for the common good. In the 7th House we find marriages, business relationships, contracts, legalities, negotiations, and agreements. Refer to page 164 for additional characteristics of the Astrological Houses.

The chakra related to Libra is the Heart Chakra – Thymus gland (high heart). The Thymus gland is located just above and to the right of the heart chakra between the heart and throat chakras. It connects emotions of Divine love, compassion, truth, and forgiveness with the area where language originates – allowing us to speak from the heart. This is the area of the etheric heart, and emphasizes selflessness and spiritual love. It creates a bridge between the physical body and soul. The thymus gland is one of the earliest glands developed in the fetus. It supports the immune function and has within it the patterning of our DNA, and information related to karmic residue, including past life information. Gently tapping on the chest will stimulate and clear blockages in the thymus gland.

The Libra new moon is a good time to stretch our mind, body, and spirit. We can do this by purifying our living space, glam up the wardrobe, or take a weekend retreat with like-minded people. Libra helps us find balance within personal relationships by helping us listen to others. It's also a good time to be a peacemaker and work for justice, especially related to whatever issues are important to you. So let your voice be heard.

Libra New Moon Questions:
What is tipping the scales out of balance?
How can I find more peace and harmony?
What relationships can I forgive and heal?
What can I do to create more beauty?
How can I cooperate and relate to other people better?
How can I reflect love and beauty back to others?
How can I listen to others more intently?

Libra New Moon Intentions

For example: I am so grateful that I live a balanced life.

_____

_____

_____

_____

_____

_____

_____

_____

Act "as if" dialogue of your intentions:

For example: I am so thrilled to be in a healthy, happy, compatible relationship with my soul mate. There has been tremendous healing take place within both of us get me to this point. We have worked through so many difficult issues and as a result, we have learned and grown with each other. Our relationship is balanced and free of power struggles. It's so awesome to feel open, trusting, loving, and loved.

_____

_____

_____

_____

_____

_____

_____

Create an empowering question or mantra:

Empowering Question Example: Why is it so easy for me to maintain balanced relationships?

Mantra Example: I easily balance all aspects of my life and enjoy life fully!

Aries Full Moon

September or October

THE ARIES – LIBRA AXIS reminds us to find balance between our individual needs (Aries) and other people's needs (Libra).

Aries represents the self. It's a great full moon to evaluate "who am I?" and discover "why am I here?" This is a good time to set our intentions on self-love and healthy self-care. When we in a place of healthy self-love, we are more available to love others and give of ourselves. When we come from a healthy place of self-love, we are authentic and powerful.

There may be particular habits or patterns brought to light that occur in relationships. This information is helpful in letting go of habits that no longer serve our highest good or path. The full moon will help in transforming behaviors.

Trust and surrender are called for now. Ultimately evolution and wholeness are achieved when we integrate our opposites and take back projections we have put onto others. This lunation gives us the perfect opportunity to let go of the past and move into the future. It will take some work on our part, but it will be worth it.

In opposition of the Aries full moon we have Libra. Libra's focus is on relationships and balance. We have relationships with everything – ourselves, our Creator, our partner, children, co-workers, boss, clients, work, money, health, environment, and anything else. Ultimately we realize we cannot control everything we have relationships with, but we can chose how we respond to those relationships. With Libra, it's time to evaluate these relationships to see what is working, and what needs to change. When relationships are working, they make us stronger. When they don't work, the relationship breaks down or falls apart.

Follow your heart and strengthen your relationship with yourself and be aware of your relationship with all aspects of your life during the Aries full moon.

During the full moon take note of impulsive behaviors. This full moon provides the intention of transformation and resolution. Fuel your imagination by creating something new. Follow the path that is illuminated as emotional issues are brought to light. As emotions arise, we want to acknowledge and release them. Creating a ritual around releasing them is a helpful tool. Here are a couple of suggestions:

1) Write down emotions, situations, beliefs, and people you wish to release, then burn the list allowing the smoke to carry the old away.
2) Use breath work using the inhale as a cleansing breath, and the exhale to release the old.
3) Use essential oils such as lime and ginger over the tailbone; or use frankincense and ylang ylang over the heart. Feel free to use other essential oils you feel drawn to use. Your body knows what it needs. Also refer to the Aries or Libra New Moon chapters for additional essential oil suggestions.

Whenever we release something it's best to replace it with what we want. The time between the full moon and the next new moon is a perfect time to go through the release and replace process. This is a purification process. It's bringing to light and being aware of our thoughts, emotions, behavior, and beliefs so we make sure they are aligned with universal truth. When we consistently release inaccurate information, we allow wholeness and the pure Divine essence of our soul to be revealed.

Purification takes place on a physical, mental, emotional, and spiritual level. It represents the means through which each soul can recognize and return to the divinity that lies within.

Find balance with the Aries full moon by honoring the emotions that arise and following your passions. Follow your passions to fulfill you soul's desires. Ultimately passion is the spice of life that is the basis of power and supports us in creating the life we desire.

Aries Full Moon Questions to Ponder:

How do I expand my creative energy?
What am I passionate about? How can I fuel my passion?
How can I more deeply connect with my spiritual self?
How do I find balance between my personal needs and balancing relationships with other people?

Full Moon Release & Reclaim
I release:

_____

_____

I reclaim:

Scorpio New Moon

October or November

Scorpio asks, "What do I Transform?"

<u>Scorpio Keywords</u>
Probing * Perceptive * Deep * Focused * Resourceful * Intense Accountability * Responsibility * Research * Self-examination * Intimacy * Self- Mastery * Change * Re-birth * Transformation Passion * Strength * Commitment * Sex * Hidden Aspects * Power * Secrets * Karma * Death * Renewal * Spiritual Growth

Element: Water - fixed
Chakra: 5th Chakra – Throat Chakra
Essential Oil Recommendations:
- Lavender
- Cilantro
- Frankincense
- Basil
- Juniper Berry
- Black Pepper

THE SCORPIO NEW MOON energy is intense, probing, passionate, perceptive, resourceful, and deep. There is nothing easy about it. The Scorpio New Moon helps us strip away the facades and find truth. It is a good moon to focus on skills of self-mastery.

Scorpio encourages us to dig deep into our personal mysteries. Any hidden aspects that need to be resolved are at the forefront of the healing agenda. This includes resolving issues related to addiction, control, intimacy, money, and power. There may be some supercharged emotions lurking around those issues, so beware of deep emotions cropping up.

There is a feeling of restlessness with Scorpio. It wants to get the work done. However, when transformation is taking place there are difficult decisions to be made, or personal crises that push us to make necessary changes.

Scorpio rules the 8th House – The House of Sex. Areas of interest in this house surround relationships and interactions that take on a communal nature. It speaks to what our relationships will bring us and how we can get the most out of them.

Shared resources fall within the 8th House. This includes inheritance, alimony, taxes, insurance and support from others. Financial support, as well as spiritual support, emotional support, and physical support are addressed by this house. Refer to page 164 for additional characteristics of the Astrological Houses.

Scorpio relates to the throat chakra – the 5th chakra. This is located in indentation just above the sternum and below the Adam's apple. It is the center of communication and expression. This chakra is responsible for speaking, as well as listening to people. Speaking our authentic desires and truth is a vital part of the healing and manifesting process.

The throat chakra also represents our personal voice, willpower, and surrendering our will to Divine will. It clarifies and purifies what is right and wrong for each of us. It helps us form the authentic truth in our belief system and enables us to be assertive in expressing that truth to others.

Imbalances in this chakra physically show up as issues in the throat, sore throat, laryngitis, colds, ear issues, mouth issues, thyroid issues, jaw, upper lungs, fatigue, stress, allergies, coughing, and stuffy nose. Using essential oils on the throat, along with speaking our truth, affirmations or visualizing balance in the chakra helps restore harmony.

When functioning harmoniously, we are able to openly express thoughts and feelings; live creatively, imaginatively, trust our inner guidance, pass along knowledge, and have a good sense of timing and rhythm.

The primary fear with the throat chakra is to communicate and be heard.

Scorpio always brings the darker lesson home. We get to meet the lovely shadows of fear, control, possessiveness, and jealousy head on. This new moon reminds us that we can get the lessons and do the Scorpio work, completely revamping ourselves. Scorpio is all about the extreme metamorphosis.

Scorpio New Moon Questions to Ponder:
What cycles of death and rebirth am I experiencing?
How can I deepen my relationship with myself and others?
What personal resources need my attention?
How do I see myself transforming?
What committed relationships can I deepen?

Scorpio New Moon Intentions

For example: I am so grateful that I easily transform myself and release the hidden issues that no longer serve me.

_____
_____
_____
_____
_____
_____
_____
_____
_____

Act "as if" dialogue of your intentions:

For example: The years of deep healing work has paid off. No longer are my emotions running the show. I feel so empowered by all the transformations my life has taken. It hasn't been easy, but I've learned to overcome some incredible fears. As a result, I feel empowered, I have strong relationships with people I value, and I feel comfortable with who I am.

_____
_____
_____
_____
_____
_____
_____

Create an empowering question or mantra:

Empowering Question Example: Why is it so easy for me to clear out unnecessary baggage?

Mantra Example: It's easy to honor myself.

Taurus Full Moon

October or November

THE TAURUS – SCORPIO AXIS reminds us to find balance between what we value (Taurus) and what we need to release (Scorpio). Taurus focuses on security, resourcefulness, and possessions. Its practical energy brings us back to earth and what we can experience with our earthly senses. Taurus reflects how we experience our self-worth.

This full moon reflects what we value most, where our true wealth lies, where our worth lies, and what sustains us. This full moon is a time to determine just what we stand for, and what we want to enhance.

Scorpio supports us in letting go. It reminds us to look deeply and closely at anything that diminishes our self-worth. Any issues related to lack in intimacy, buried beliefs in scarcity, and the inability to show up in all of our glory are dug up by Scorpios deep, probing energy.

We are seeing how to fundamentally surrender to the Divine for our survival. This is emphasized in the 5th Chakra, which is influenced by Scorpio. We can only surrender to Divine will when we feel secure within our personal power, which is governed by our 2nd chakra.

During the full moon, follow the path that is illuminated as you work though emotional issues brought up. As emotions arise, we want to acknowledge and release them. Creating a ritual around releasing them is a helpful tool. Here are a couple of suggestions:

1) Write down emotions, situations, beliefs, and people you wish to release, then burn the list (in a safe manner) allowing the smoke to carry the old away.
2) Use breath work using the inhale as a cleansing breath, and the exhale to release the old.
3) Use essential oils such as bergamot, coriander, cinnamon, or grapefruit over the second chakra. This supports a healthy self-worth and boosts self confidence. Feel free to use other essential oils you feel drawn to use. Your body knows what it needs. Also refer to the Taurus or Scorpio New Moon chapters for additional essential oil suggestions.

Whenever we release something it's best to replace it with what we want. The time between the full moon and the next new moon is a perfect time to go through the release and replace process. This is a purification process. Which means we are aware of our thoughts, emotions, behavior, and beliefs, so we make sure they are aligned with universal truth. When we consistently release inaccurate information, we allow wholeness and the pure Divine essence of our soul to be revealed.

Purification takes place on a physical, mental, emotional, and spiritual level. It represents the means through which each soul can recognize and return to the divinity that lies within.

Find balance with the Taurus full moon by honoring the emotions that arise and determining what you value most. Allow your values to align with your soul's desires. Ultimately what we value, and have passion for supports our personal power and leading the life we desire.

Taurus Full Moon Thought Provoking Questions:
What do I value?
How do I value myself?
How do I surrender my will to Divine will?
What do I stand for?
Where does my true wealth and worth lie?
Where can I trust more?
Where can I be more grounded?

Full Moon Release & Reclaim
I release:

_____

_____

_____

_____

_____

_____

_____

_____

_____

_____

I reclaim:

Sagittarius New Moon

November or December

Sagittarius asks, "What do I Envision?"

<u>Sagittarius Keywords</u>
Imagination * Expansive * Adventurous * Visionary * Spirited * Independent * Optimistic * Courageous * Faithful * Confident Spontaneous * Passionate * Outgoing * Instinctive * Honest * Philosophical * Enthusiasm * Risk * Radiance * Cheerful * Sincere * Kind-Hearted * Freedom Loving * Intellectual * Fun

Element: Fire - mutable
Chakra: 6th Chakra – The Zeal Point – base of the brainstem
Essential Oil Recommendations:
- Frankincense
- Lemon
- Roman Chamomile
- Sandalwood
- Geranium
- Black Pepper

SAGITTARIUS SUPPORTS OUR QUEST for expansion. It helps us expand our horizons through its optimism, enthusiasm, independence and its adventurous nature. We enhance our ability to manifest with this fiery energy pushing us.

Fire signs inspire us to take action. Think of it as "Spirit in Motion." While working with this fire energy, there may be sudden illuminating flashes of insight and bursts of enthusiasm. Just like fire, with Sagittarius there can be inspirational flares that move ideas into action. There is a willingness to take risks because the fire energy inspires trust in life's journey. When divine inspiration sparks during this new moon, ideas may spread like wildfire.

Sagittarius helps us detach from fears so we gain a different perspective. It helps us let go of mundane details and find the courage to break out of the box. It supports our ability to have faith, hope, and inspired vision. As perceptions shift, we gain confidence, clarity, and insight into the next step. Fire is a purifier. It cleanses the old to make room for the new.

Sagittarius encourages us to be bold, look at the bigger picture, and to dream big. We may not be able to achieve all of our visions during this lunar cycle, but it provides insight into new possibilities. Because Sagittarius thinks in big terms, there may be a tendency to over-commit. Let go of frustrations if ideas don't come to fruition in the next month. Changes take place in the right time frame. Be patient, and allow the ideas to percolate. Who knows where these new ideas will lead in the New Year.

Sagittarius rules the 9th House – The House of Philosophy. In this house there is a search for meaning or understanding our world through exploring. Through higher education, we have the hope of understanding concepts and theories that enhance our world. The 9th House reminds us that we are on a voyage of discovery. Along the way we face lessons, our ideals, and the unknown that shape our ethics and beliefs. The 9th House influences long distance travel and experiencing different cultures and people. The 9th House is best described as philosophically searching for truth and meaning.

Sagittarius influences the zeal point chakra located on the back of the head at the base of the brainstem. It helps us in releasing energy that collects and becomes stuck in the head. It assists us in speaking our truth. When optimized, this chakra has the ability to express the fully conscious mind and spiritual powers through the voice. Refer to page 164 for additional characteristics of the Astrological Houses.

This energy center helps us awaken and activate all of our energy centers and align with our authentic self. This chakra is a 4th dimension chakra, where the primary chakras, one through seven, are 3rd dimensional chakras. This means we are able to hold higher frequencies of light which allows the physical body and spiritual body to ascend. As each of the 4th dimensional chakras become stable and balanced, we become open to higher levels of spiritual evolvement.

Sagittarius revives our weary soul and puts a twinkle back into our eyes. With this new moon seek out an inspired vision, one that is ignited by passion, ideas, and enthusiasm. See the bigger picture, unique mission, and personal gifts you have to share with the world. Sagittarius helps us be loyal to our own sense of what is true.

Sagittarius New Moon Questions to Ponder:
What is my natural rhythm and timing?
How do I trust my inner guidance more?
Where can I be more expressive, creative, and imaginative?

How can I effectively communicate my truth?

Sagittarius New Moon Intentions
For example: I easily follow inspired action to push boldly towards my goals.

_____

_____

_____

_____

_____

_____

_____

_____

Act "as if" dialogue of your intentions:

For example: I am so inspired! The new programs and tools I launched in the beginning of 2016 have been absolutely amazing. I called to share my success with Suzanne, who during a brilliant brainstorming session helped me create these incredible new products and promotional items to up-level my amazing client's results. They synergy that the Sagittarius energy created has launched life to the next level. People are calling me and sending messages to let me know how these tools and classes help them overcome issues and achieve what they desire in a shorter period of time. So amazing that simple bursts of insight provide for all of our intentions.

_____

_____

_____

Create an empowering question or mantra:

Empowering Question Example: Why is it so easy for me to follow my inspiration and follow the fire within?

Mantra Example: Inspiration and flow are the way I go

Gemini Full Moon

November or December

THE GEMINI – SAGITTARIUS AXIS helps us find balance between the lower or conscious mind (Gemini) and higher mind or unconscious and super conscious (Sagittarius).

The Gemini Full moon is a lighthearted airy energy that is interested in moving ideas and communication forward. This includes projects related to speaking, teaching, and writing. It does this through networks, social media, and socializing.

Communication expands our presence in the world. Through communicating ideas, we express our wisdom, and whatever we are passionate about. Gemini rules our communication skills, the conscious mind, speaking, and listening. It also influences our intellect, perceptions, and thought patterns.

Gemini gives us a pause from the deep spiritual growth and striving cycles we've been in for the past several months. It asks us to celebrate accomplishments, acknowledge growth, and be grateful for the lessons. Our internal growth is just as vital as external accomplishments. No matter how big or small our accomplishments seem, we need to take time to pat ourselves on the back and honor ourselves. The more we celebrate and focus on what is working, the more good things we attract or magnetize to us. We magnify whatever we focus on. This energy comes back to us in unexpected opportunities, new adventures, better relationships, more money, and improved health.

Gemini full moon may bring brilliant breakthroughs. There is a magic with this moon that helps us seed the New Year. Keep in mind we can change anything whether it's our health, money, or relationship issues. Everything is within our power to change.

When we take responsibility for what is happening in our lives, we can transmute it through conscious choices to create new thought patterns and habits. This process becomes easier when we call in the power of our Creator to assist us.

Sagittarius supports and expands this full moon. It helps us tap into the higher mind, spiritual consciousness, Divine source, expansion of consciousness, inspiration, and joy. As a fire sign, it wants to take action and supports us in getting what we want. Sagittarius takes all that we are and expands it throughout the work asking questions such as, "Where can I take this idea?"

With expansion, attitude is everything. It is the pump that drives it all. With Gemini the focus is on the power of the mind. Through consciousness we change everything. The power of the mind heals the body, strengthens the spirit, and enhances the mind + body + spirit connection.

We can use this energy to uplift ourselves, be empowered, and bring in more of what we want in the New Year. Through an "attitude of gratitude" and appreciation we receive more.

When we focus on always giving life our best, we receive the best in return. It may show up in unexpected ways and opportunities – things that seem to be out of the blue. It is simply our job to always, always, always do our best.

During the full moon notice any opportunities to be more social and expressive. Follow the path that expands these areas. As emotions and fears are brought to light, take time to acknowledge them in a playful, spontaneous way – such as through humor. Life becomes easier when we can learn to laugh at ourselves. As emotions arise, we want to acknowledge and release them. Creating a ritual around releasing them is a helpful tool. Here are a couple of suggestions:

1) Write down emotions, situations, beliefs, and people you wish to release, then burn the list (in a safe manner) allowing the smoke to carry the old away.
2) Use breath work using the inhale as a cleansing breath, and the exhale to release the old.
3) Use essential oils such as lavender, wild orange, bergamot, cinnamon or grapefruit over the 2nd chakra. Feel free to use other essential oils you feel drawn to. Your body knows what it needs. Also refer to the Gemini or Sagittarius New Moon chapters for additional essential oil suggestions.

Whenever we release something it's best to replace it with what we want. The time between the full moon and the next new moon is a perfect time to go through the release and replace process. This is a purification process. Through conscious awareness of our thoughts, emotions, behavior, and beliefs, we can shift any incorrect ones so they are aligned with universal truth. When we consistently release inaccurate information, we allow wholeness and the pure Divine essence of our soul to be revealed.

Purification takes place on a physical, mental, emotional, and spiritual level. It represents the means through which each soul can recognize and return to the divinity that lies within.

Find balance with the Gemini full moon by honoring the emotions and fears that arise. Express emotions and fears in a healthy way. This mindfulness helps switch gears, and break old patterns. Consciousness is heightened with the mental energy of Gemini. Over the next few weeks it's important to be mindful of daily interactions on all levels of connection and awareness.

Gemini Full Moon Questions to Ponder:
What am I ready to change to enhance how I communicate, network, and socialize with other people?
How can I be more playful and engaging with other people?
How do I use my sensory abilities to navigate my life?
Do I feel overwhelmed by energy around me?
Am I using escape through food, alcohol or other addictions to mask sensory overload?
How do I stand in my power and create the life I crave?

Full Moon Release & Reclaim
I release:

_____
_____
_____
_____
_____
_____
_____

I reclaim:

Capricorn New Moon

December or January

Capricorn asks, "Who Am I in the World?"

<u>Capricorn Keywords</u>

Structure * Foundation * Inner Authority * Reputation * Respect * Responsibility * Life's Purpose * Material Security * Authority * Ambition * Hard Work * Discipline * Prestige * Self-Sufficiency * Contribution * Public Persona * Reliability *

Element: Earth - Cardinal
Chakra: 1st Chakra – Third Eye – Brow Chakra
Essential Oil Recommendations:
- Lavender
- Frankincense
- Roman Chamomile
- Sandalwood
- Clary Sage
- Coriander
- Fennel

CAPRICORN IS A CARDINAL EARTH SIGN. Cardinal signs are the ones that push us forward. They initiate and forge ahead with plans. They are the instigators and attract those that support their efforts. As we work with the Capricorn energy, we are all influenced by this positive, forward thrust. Capricorn being an earth sign provides a grounded presence and a natural authority of mastering life on a physical plane. The cardinal signs kick off each of the seasons. Capricorn is the first new moon of winter.

Capricorn is symbolically portrayed as the mountain goat steadily ascending to the top of the peak. It represents the ability for us to reach our highest intentions, climbing towards our higher self. When we learn who we are and what gifts we are here to share with humanity, we show the world *"who am I in the world?"* This is reflected in the work we do or our career.

Capricorn is constructive, resourceful, disciplined, wise, ambitious, consistent, and prudent. Each of us is responsible for creating, maintaining, and sustaining our own lives. Capricorn encourages us to initiate, manage and have authority over our own life.

Capricorn is the foundation of our home, work, food, and shelter. It helps us address issues related to physical and emotional security. With the Capricorn New Moon, find areas that inspire and create passion within. When we align our purpose and work, life becomes more meaningful.

Capricorn also reminds us of our responsibility for our thoughts, emotions, beliefs, behavior, and understanding how all of this connects to our physical reality. These fundamental elements are vital in manifesting more. When thoughts and beliefs are inaccurate, we create a reality that is distorted. A foundation must be based on Universal Truth to be sustainable.

By building inner strength, fortifying existing foundations, and creating sustainable systems, our outer reality become more stable, organized, methodical, and efficient. Inner strength comes from believing in ourselves, acknowledging your successes, and using them as benchmarks to continue on our path.

Capricorn rules our life's work. We are each given unique gifts that support humanity. Unfortunately, few people follow those passions believing they will not be able to financially sustain themselves. But we are moving into a place where we turn our faith to the Divine to provide guidance into developing our talents to share with humanity. As we do what we love, we will be financially supported. We need to get out of logically thinking of how we need to make money and begin asking our inner guidance how to receive it.

Money and wealth are a big part of the Capricorn energy since it rules our career and social status. We have been raised in a society that processes life primarily from logic versus intuition. We literally have to overcome our personal perceptions and family beliefs of how to make money. Also there is the scarcity beliefs that are prevalent in each of our DNA. This occurs because each of us have had ancestors that have experienced some sort of scarcity. Beliefs are passed down generation after generation through coding in our DNA. Although you may not have personally experienced scarcity, it still may be in your genes. The good news is you can change it.

When there are ancestor related issues and patterns that come up, practice the release exercise similar to the full moon chapters. We release the emotions from our lifetime and our ancestor's lifetimes, replacing the old with thriving success, abundance, or other desired result.

Awareness of our thoughts, beliefs, actions, and patterns related to money helps us reprogram the subconscious by removing the old patterns and creating a new one. It takes practice and continuous awareness into our thoughts, emotions, and behaviors to make these changes. But once resolved, we operate from the new programming, helping us attract more.

In resolving beliefs and emotional wounds of our ancestors, we release the chains that bind us to the past. It raises our vibration. It also raises the vibration of the planet, because any emotion that is created here on earth has to be resolved on this earthly plane.

Capricorn relates to the 10th House – The House of Social Status. Vocation is a big part of the 10th House. Our career or profession reflects how we see ourselves contributing to society. Career development, goals, ambition, and motivation are all a part of the 10th House. This House reflects how our social status is achieved as a result of our career. How we use these gifts and the status that comes along with them is important. The bigger question is, "Will we use this power to enhance society or is it self-serving? Our relationship as the individual and how it relates to the group or society is heightened in the 10th House. Refer to page 164 for additional characteristics of the Astrological Houses.

Capricorn is associated with the Third Eye or Brow Chakra. This chakra is located in the center of the head. It connects us to our internal intuition, sharpens our senses, has the ability to read the future, and receive non-verbal messages. Through the Third Eye we communicate with the world and our Divine source.

It influences the face, ears, eyes, nose, sinuses, and nervous system. Imbalances show up as headaches, hormonal imbalance, nervous tension, difficulty concentrating, sleep disturbances, difficulty in making decisions, sinus congestion, foggy brain, pain in the eyes, depression, and slow thinking. When harmonious, this chakra enhances our intuition, perceptions, and imagination. We receive insight about the world and how to live more efficiently. We think and live holistically with nature. We demonstrate advanced intellectual skills, and integrate information on many different levels enhancing our contributions to society. The brow chakra helps us release illusion because we all have the right to see truth.

Capricorn inspires us to get to work and expand our career by following our heart's desires. With this new moon, put into action the inspired dreams that took place with Sagittarius new moon and follow our passion.

Capricorn New Moon Questions to Ponder:
Do I have a solid foundation aligned with Universal truth?
What lessons am I being tested on now?
Have I given my inner authority away?
How can I take my authority back?
What is my purpose or life's path?
Do I currently perform work I am passionate about?
Am I following my heart's desires?
How committed am I to stability and endurance?
How do I define material success?

Capricorn New Moon Intentions
For example: I am so grateful that I am passionate about the rewarding work I do that provides a consistent income stream that financially empowers me, and supports my family.

_____

_____

Act "as if" dialogue of your intentions:

For example: I'm so thrilled that the work supports my inner passion. I am confident and easily stand in my power. There is nothing to prove to anyone. I am following my heart's desire. As a result, I am standing in a flow on infinite success. I easily manifest my goals and dreams instantly. It feels good to stand at the top of the mountain and look over what I've achieved. I'm so grateful that I get to empower other people with this knowledge and wisdom. Watching them grow and succeed is so rewarding.

Create an empowering question or mantra:

Empowering Question Example: Why is it so easy for me to expand my gifts that serve humanity and support me?

Mantra Example: Following my life's purpose is easy.

Cancer Full Moon

December or January

THE CANCER – CAPRICORN AXIS reminds us to find balance between the emotional body (Cancer) and social structure and physical reality (Capricorn). The Cancer full moon turns our focus to nurturing and caring for others as well as ourselves. It is compassionate, loving, and kind. It is the archetype of the Mother.

As a water sign, Cancer helps us dive beneath the surface and determine the emotional wounds that are lurking in our psyche. Cancer evaluates life through feelings. It is empathic and picks up the mood of the room. Look at emotions that are surfacing to determine if they are personal or belong to someone else.

The Cancer full moon makes us aware of how well our rules and social structures fulfill their purpose. It encourages us to pay attention to our real needs and passions so that we align with our soul's purpose.

The Capricorn sun encourages us to take authority in our lives related to career, money, and how we make our way in the world. When we identify what our needs and passions are and no longer sleep-walk through life as a servant of patriarchy and consumerism, we step into our higher-self. Capricorn represents our highest achievement – becoming self-actualized and enlightened. Our passion becomes our career and contribution to humanity.

Cancer represents the mother, while Capricorn represents the father. This duality may crop up in areas of our life where there is still a struggle between finding our true power and balancing the masculine/feminine energies.

Finding balance between our inner world (Cancer) and the outer world (Capricorn) is necessary so the scales are not tipped too far in either direction. We are at a crossroads of consciousness. Do we revert back to old ways of thinking and processing life or do we step into our power and actually create the life we crave?

During the full moon, follow the path that is illuminated as you work though emotional issues brought up. As emotions arise, we want to acknowledge and release them. Creating a ritual around releasing them is a helpful tool. Here are a couple of suggestions:

1) Write down emotions, situations, beliefs, and people you wish to release, then burn the list (in a safe manner) allowing the smoke to carry the old away.
2) Use breath work using the inhale as a cleansing breath, and the exhale to release the old.
3) Use essential oils such as geranium, white fir, and/or Ylang Ylang over the heart. I personally love this combination to release issues related to trust, resolving ancestral patterns stuck in the DNA, and restore optimism to the heart. Using frankincense (father and authority issues) and/or myrrh (mother and nurturing

issues) along with white fir over the heart or along the spine supports balancing the masculine and feminine energies within. Feel free to use other essential oils you feel drawn to. Your body knows what it needs. Also, refer to the Capricorn or Cancer New Moon chapters for additional essential oil suggestions.

Whenever we release something it's best to replace it with what we want. The time between the full moon and the next new moon is a perfect time to go through the release and replace process. This is the purification process. Which basically means we are aware of our thoughts, emotions, behavior, and beliefs and make sure they are aligned with universal truth. When we consistently release inaccurate information, we allow wholeness and the pure Divine essence of our soul to be revealed.

Purification takes place on a physical, mental, emotional, and spiritual level. It represents the means through which each soul can recognize and return to the divinity that lies within.

Find balance with the Cancer full moon by honoring the emotions that arise and following your passions. Find ways to allow your passions to follow the soul's desires. Ultimately, passion is the basis of power and supports us in creating the life we desire.

Cancer Full Moon Questions to Ponder:
How do I find balance between caring for myself, others and social status?
Am I creating an energy rich reality for myself, family, and community?
How can I nurture myself in new innovative ways this year?

What changes am I ready to implement now to create a holistic approach to life?

What lessons have I learned in the last year that prepare me for the changes of the New Year?

Full Moon Release & Reclaim

I release:

_____
_____
_____
_____
_____
_____
_____
_____
_____
_____

I reclaim:

_____
_____
_____
_____
_____
_____
_____
_____

Aquarius New Moon

January or February

Aquarius asks, "What Wisdom Can I Share?"

<u>Aquarius Keywords</u>
Humanitarian * Honest * Eccentric * Futuristic * Original * Inventive * Independent * Unconventional * Willful * Collective Conscious * Freedom * Spirit * Equality * Groups Community * Collaboration * Networking * Clarity * Awakening * Expanding Consciousness * Collective Efforts

Element: Air - fixed
Chakra: 6th Chakra – Pineal Gland
Essential Oil Recommendations:
- Clary Sage
- Melissa
- Roman Chamomile
- Cedarwood
- Lemon
- Ginger

AQUARIUS IS AN AIR SIGN. Air signs typically use their minds to make sense of life. There may be an element of justifying life with this Aquarius new moon. As a fixed air sign, Aquarius is able to follow one train of thought. Air signs can elevate our ideas and free-thinking by offering a different spin on how to prioritize things.

Aquarius is symbolized as the water bearer. Aquarius pours its knowledge over humanity. It strives for bettering humanity – envisioning freedom, equality, and building community for everyone. Its emphasis is on the group mind, ideas, and working together.

On a deeper level, the Aquarius energy is interested in awakening the mind and its vast potential – urging us to strive for true freedom. The Age of Aquarius is rooted in humanity living consciously. As we each do our part in living consciously, we raise the collective conscious and those who are unaware or unwilling to do the necessary healing work also benefit.

The Aquarius new moon supports expanding our vision for the greater good. Networking and group activities are a great place to focus efforts this lunar cycle. Participating in brainstorming with others that supports like-minded pursuits would be a great activity with the Aquarius energy. Collaboration strengthens ties and expands ideas that support our goals and the evolution of humanity.

The Aquarius new moon is a good time to take risks and activities that require bold action, and originality. It supports the visionary within each of us as we "see" the bigger picture. Activities that expand the mental and intuitive elements of us are encouraged with this new moon.

There may be an inner restlessness or heightened awareness to connect with other people during the new moon. Any goals related to making connections, joining forces with others – both personally and professionally are supported at this time.

Aquarius supports being on the forefront of new ideas; it is the mental pioneer. There is a tendency to focus on the present and future versus dwelling on the past. Remember that whatever we consistently focus on we attract. To catch our next blessing we need to let go of the baggage.

Aquarius rules the 11th House – the House of Friends. In this house we find strength in numbers. This includes clubs, organizations, social groups, and associations. With the collective group, we can achieve more. There is a heightened awareness of our position in life within the context of the group, rather than through self-centered focus. The 11th house brings us allies, the comforts of shared experiences, and the strength of a collective stand. It represents the social codes that bind a society and the revolutions that break them apart. It is a future-oriented house, but also has threads that tie us to the past. The 11th House is where we receive love. It is the house of hope and dreams. Refer to page 164 for additional characteristics of the Astrological Houses.

Aquarius also influences the pineal gland chakra. It is related to the 6th chakra, and has an integral part of spiritual awakening and intuition. It is a small endocrine gland located in the center of the brain. It produces melatonin, a hormone that affects wake/sleep patterns and seasonal functions.

It is known in esoteric teachings for its connection between the physical and spiritual worlds. The pineal gland has always been important in initiating supernatural powers. Development of psychic talents has been closely associated with this gland of higher vision. It is associated with the Third Eye, which is a lens that opens to see beyond physical reality. When the Third Eye opens, it can feel like a pressure at the base of the brain.

Increasing our intuitive gifts improves our connection with our Higher-self.

Imbalances in Third Eye chakra may result in headaches or pressure in the head, eye problems, nightmares, and lack of insight. Frankincense is a great essential oil to support the pineal gland because it crosses the blood/brain barrier. Place a drop of oil on the tongue and press against the roof of the mouth. When balanced, the pineal gland enhances our intuitions, perceptions, and imagination. There is an increase in information and insight into the world; we think and live holistically with nature and we have advanced intellectual skills.

Aquarius New Moon Questions to Ponder:
Where can I live more consciously?
What is my purpose or mission?
Am I following my intuition or inner wisdom?
How can I collaborate to enhance my mission or purpose?
What is my highest vision for my life?

Aquarius New Moon Intentions

For example: I am so grateful to be collaborating with other successful entrepreneurs who are supporting the professional development of holistic healers.

_____
_____
_____
_____
_____
_____

Act "as if" dialogue of your intentions:

For example: What a thrilling day. My Holistic Business Development program was a huge success! People are seeing the results of the collaborative effort this program created. Their businesses are expanding beyond their wildest dreams. Offers to collaborate with several people I admire have been coming in. I'm so excited to be working with some very influential and successful people. It is so gratifying to see how everything is effortlessly coming together and seeing the difference this is making in many people's lives.

Create an empowering question or mantra Aquarius intentions:

Empowering Question Example: Why is it so easy to see my life's mission? Why is it so easy to see my vision with clarity?

Mantra Example: I am attuned to my vision.

Leo Full Moon

January or February

THE LEO – AQUARIUS AXIS focuses on striking balance between what is personal (Leo) and what is impersonal (Aquarius). Leo is the king of the jungle. He has nothing to fear. Leo is creative, passionate, dramatic, spontaneous, and boosts the individual ego through playfulness. The Aquarius sun focuses on the group mind, impersonal relationships, and finding solutions and equality for everyone.

Leo wants to be more than just a team player. It wants to let its light shine. You may be inspired to take a new direction or have creative insight into your existing goals that lead you closer to success. Use this insight as an opportunity to grow, knowing that whatever is coming up may not necessarily be rational.

The desires of the heart move us in mysterious ways. The brain can't always make sense of the inner pull that occurs in the heart or what passions are fueled. The Leo full moon magnifies our passions and what drives us to be successful.

It's important for us to love ourselves more than the need for a relationship. When we seek love and approval outside of ourselves, we tend to give in or give up part of ourselves to be in the relationship. When we love ourselves and stand in our power, there is no need to give power away as a compromise to being in the relationship. Leo reminds us to be true to ourselves. When we love ourselves, we attract relationships that honor our authentic self.

Typically, the full moon is directed outward to manifest intentions set with the new moon; however, this full moon is directed inward and is reflective of what really drives us.

Full moons show us how to use the complimentary energies of the opposite astrological signs. They help us become aware of something new about ourselves and the world.

During the full moon, be introspective and notice what makes you feel alive and where you perform well. As emotions and fears arise, acknowledge and release them to the sun. The sun rules Leo and is a powerful energy incinerator. Create a ritual around releasing emotions. Here are a couple of suggestions:

1) Write down emotions, situations, beliefs, and people you wish to release, then burn the list (in a safe manner) allowing the smoke to carry the old away.
2) Envision your list of fears or emotions allowing the sun's rays to incinerate them.
3) Use breath work using the inhale as a cleansing breath, and the exhale to release the old.
4) Use essential oils such as wild orange, ylang ylang, or rosemary, lemon, or bergamot over the 3rd chakra – Solar Plexus or along the spine. Feel free to use other essential oils you feel drawn to use. Your body knows what it needs. Also refer to the Leo or Aquarius New Moon chapters for additional essential oil suggestions.

Whenever we release something it's best to replace it with what we want. The time between the full moon and the next new moon is a perfect time to go through the release and replace process. This is a purification process. Which mean we are very aware of our thoughts, emotions, behavior, and beliefs so we make sure they are aligned with universal truth. When we consistently release inaccurate information, we allow wholeness and the pure Divine essence of our soul to be revealed.

Purification takes place on a physical, mental, emotional, and spiritual level. It represents the means through which each soul can recognize and return to the divinity that lies within.

Find balance with the Leo full moon by honoring the emotions that arise and following your passions. Be expressive, fun, and generous. Use charisma and natural warmth to expand communication and what you love in life. Find ways to allow your passions to follow the soul's desires. Ultimately passion is the basis of power and supports us in creating the life we desire.

Leo Full Moon Questions to Ponder:
Where do I feel love and passion in my life?
How can I enhance self-love?
Do I authentically stand in my power?
Where am I giving my power away?
Where can I be more fun and child-like?
How can I awaken my heart's desires?
How can I express my authentic self?
How can I be more generous and giving?

Full Moon Release & Reclaim

I release:

I reclaim:

Pisces New Moon

February or March

Pisces asks, "What Do I Know?"

<u>Pisces Keywords</u>
Dreams * Vision * Imagination * Fantasy * Limitations * Creative Visualization * Surrender * Sensitivity * Duality * Compassion * Psychic Gifts * Universal Love * Empathy * Merging * Healing * Magic * Illusion * Unconscious * Unmask

Element: Water - mutable
Chakra: Crown Chakra
Essential Oil Recommendations:
- Rose
- Melissa
- Roman Chamomile
- Frankincense
- Sandalwood
- Juniper Berry & Rosemary

THE PISCES NEW MOON is a time of soul-searching. This new moon is especially inspirational, imaginative, and creative, boosting new perspectives and insight. Like all water signs, it's a time to go inward and address emotional issues that cause our lens to be out of focus. This lunar cycle supports review, letting go, and evaluating spiritual growth. During this new moon, there may be a tendency to find some level of emotional peace of mind, as well as peace within the soul. Reviewing accomplishments and changes over the last twelve months gives us a measure of success in our spiritual evolution as we end the astrological year.

Pisces is symbolically represented by two fish swimming in opposite directions. These two fish represent the duality that lies within each of us between the fully developed instinctual side and the immature spiritual nature. Ultimately, the goal is to live a unified personal and spiritual life.

Pisces is a mutable water sign. It is symbolic of the boundless ocean of unlimited possibilities. The Pisces Moon reminds us to be empathetic, kind-hearted, generous, compassionate, and to appreciate beauty. On the opposite side, Pisces may drum up fluctuating moods, hypersensitivity, indecisiveness, and doses of self-pity. The key to navigating churning emotions is compassion, balance, and accepting change.

Pisces helps us make sense of life. It helps us see how all of the pieces fit together. It rules the subconscious mind where pain and fears are stored. It holds our secrets and sorrows, and teaches us how to deal with life consciously and unconsciously. It encourages us to heal painful wounds by using spiritual tools and connecting to the Divine. In healing the past we move forward without emotional baggage.

It is the last astrological sign in the astrological year. It's an introspective time to evaluate what we have accomplished over the past year as we prepare for the new one.

There is a need to find some level of emotional peace of mind. This is a period of renewal, letting go, and recharging one's spiritual batteries. Book a retreat, spend time in nature, swim in water, spend time by a river, lake, or ocean, or take an Epsom salt bath with your favorite essential oils.

Pisces rules the 12th House – the House of the Unconscious. The Unconscious state assists us in coping with difficult situations and failures. It is the House of Reckoning since it is an opportunity to review what we have done and decide where to go from here. Within this House are also our hidden strengths and weaknesses that are concealed from the public view. Refer to page 164 for additional characteristics of the Astrological Houses.

The subconscious works hard to help us make sense of our lives. With this introspective house, we may feel stuck, bound, or confined in life. For this reason, this House rules jails, hospitals, institutions, asylums, and any place that inhibits freedom. We can overcome self-imposed limitations with the help of this House by visiting the unconscious and facing the past; in doing so we remove the chains that bind us and create a new path for the future.

Pisces influences the Crown chakra. It is located at the top of the head. Within this chakra is the power to reach complete enlightenment. It is the energy center connected to both the physical and spiritual worlds. It processes spiritual insight from the Divine filtering it into the pineal gland/third eye for integration into the physical body. It is our spiritual connection.

Imbalances in this chakra are reflected in the physical body as poor short-term memory, learning difficulties, and confusion.

This also shows up as poor coordination, ringing in the ears, and nervous system imbalances. It also may be reflected as spiritual cynicism, feeling separated from wholeness, uncertainty of our purpose, or disassociation from the body. Harmonious functions enhance our intellect, sense of spiritual connection, and the ability to perceive, analyze, and assimilate information.

As we reflect on the astrological year, we celebrate our successes and growth, and provide a fertile field for planting new seeds. Pisces is a time to rest, reflect, and prepare for the new astrological year.

Pisces New Moon Questions to Ponder:
Am I consciously living my divine purpose?
Am I open to all the goodness and abundance of the Universe?
Do I feel I am at one with all of creation?
How can I deepen my spiritual connection?
Do I feel connected to my body as well as the Divine?

Pisces New Moon Intentions
For example: I am so happy to travel to Costa Rica to share insight and celebrate my successes for the last year, as well as growth of my clients.

_____

_____

_____

_____

_____

_____

_____

Act "as if" dialogue of your intentions:

For example: Our annual retreat to Costa Rica was an amazing way to celebrate the end of the astrological year. It was an incredible year of manifesting, personal and professional growth. My projects have been a huge success and people are rapidly healing, changing, and manifesting what they want. Many of the people who participate in my programs have joined me to celebrate our growth and honor ourselves in Costa Rica. It was a very rejuvenating experience filled with shared love, admiration, laughter, and tears. I am so grateful to be part of this awesome journey and the people that have joined me.

Create an empowering question or mantra:

Empowering Question Example: Why is it so easy for me to spiritually evolve and achieve my desires and help other people do it too?

Mantra Example: My soul is fed when I serve myself and others.

Virgo Full Moon

February or March

THE VIRGO – PISCES AXIS reminds us to find balance between physical (Virgo) and emotional (Pisces) health. Virgo supports our habits around diet, exercise, and physiological health. Pisces delves into what lies behind the scenes. As a water sign, it brings to the surface unrecognized strengths, fears, and limitations that hold us back.

Full moons remind us how to find balance between opposition. It brings awareness that we need to address through external circumstances and other people. The full moon reflects hidden aspects that need our attention.

Virgo reminds us to develop daily habits and take action towards the higher vision and dreams that we create with the Pisces new moon. We honor our dreams and inner messages by taking action towards them. Virgo provides the discipline and practical persistence to achieve anything.

Virgo is symbolized as the virgin, who seeks self-knowledge and knows both the light and shadow sides of herself. The virgin concept is beyond the physical, sexual aspect. A virgin is someone who belongs to no one. She represents our personal power and it is our birthright to reclaim our power. The Virgo full moon helps us see who we are meant to be if we are willing to accept our divine self.

Although we are a part of the collective consciousness, we are each unique and contribute our soul's destiny to the whole. Virgo supports us to understand how things fit together. Her greatest gift is discernment and learning to trust inner wisdom for guidance. This in turn helps us master our talents and understand how these talents contribute to the collective whole. We learn how we can serve others with our gifts.

The Pisces sun illuminates our deep spiritual side. It helps us see how we have integrated our physical world with the spiritual one. This polarity strengthens our connection to trust in spirit while taking practical steps that are necessary to bring our goals to fruition. Pisces brings an element of truth to every thought and magnifies our intentions.

During the full moon, follow the path that is illuminated as you work though emotional issues brought up. As emotions arise, we want to acknowledge and release them. Creating a ritual around releasing them is a helpful tool. Here are a couple of suggestions:

1) Write down emotions, situations, beliefs, and people you wish to release, then burn the list (in a safe manner) allowing the smoke to carry the old away.
2) Breath work – using the inhale as a cleansing breath, and the exhale to release the old.
3) Use essential oils such as geranium, cypress, peppermint, white fir, eucalyptus, or rose oil between the Solar Plexus and heart. Feel free to use other essential oils you feel drawn to use. Your body knows

what it needs. Also refer to the Leo or Pisces New Moon chapters for additional essential oil suggestions.

Whenever we release something it's best to replace it with what we want. The time between the full moon and the next new moon is a perfect time to go through the release and replace process. This is a purification process. When we are aware of our thoughts, emotions, behavior, and beliefs, we can change them to be aligned with universal truth. As we consistently release inaccurate information, we allow wholeness and the pure Divine essence of our soul to be revealed.

Purification takes place on a physical, mental, emotional, and spiritual level. It represents the means through which each soul can recognize and return to the divinity that lies within.

Find balance with the Virgo full moon by honoring the emotions that arise and following your passion. Virgo symbolizes the potential to harmonize the practical aspects of life with the spiritual ones. Find ways to allow your passions to follow the soul's desires. Ultimately finding balance between physical needs and spiritual needs is the emphasis of this Virgo full moon.

Virgo Full Moon Questions to Ponder:

How do I take better care of my physical needs?
How do I reclaim my personal power?
What important insights about my personal habits are brought to light at this time?
How do I express high standards to honor myself?

Full Moon Release & Reclaim

I release:

I reclaim:

Conclusion

I hope you have enjoyed this year-long journey of self-discovery. Each year we begin a new astrological calendar with the Aries New Moon. Over the years, as you fill your journals with your wishes and insights, you can reflect back to prior journals to see your growth and transformation. This helps you see progress towards becoming a better version of yourself.

Each year I hope you manifest more, and move closer to the life of your dreams. Dream big and live the life you want.

It would be greatly appreciated if you leave an honest review of your experience with this book.

Wishing you a wildly abundant life
manifesting your heart's desires!

Lunar Cycle References

Each year the new and full moons take place on a different date. For a current schedule of the new and full moons visit www.NewMoonManifesting.com.

You can also join our mailing list where you will receive an email reminding you of the upcoming new and full moons. With each new moon we hold a live conference call that you're invited to participate in to learn more about manifesting. During the calls we talk about the current new moon and provide a guided imagery meditation to help you set your intentions for the new cycle.

Astrological Sign Summary

Aries asks – "Who am I?"

Taurus asks – "What do I value?"

Gemini asks – "What do I think?"

Cancer asks – "What do I feel?"

Leo asks – "What do I love?"

Virgo asks – "What do I purify?"

Libra asks – "How do I relate to others?"

Scorpio asks – "What do I transform?"

Sagittarius asks – "What do I envision?"

Capricorn asks – "Who am I in the world?"

Aquarius asks – "What wisdom can I share?"

Pisces asks – "What do I know?"

Astrological House Descriptions

1st House of Self – Beginnings, physical appearance, body image, traits, first impressions, general outlook of the world, reinvent oneself, personal habits

2nd House of Wealth – Material and immaterial things of value, belongings, acquisitions, growth, cultivation, self-worth, five senses, attunement to the physical world, financial concerns

3rd House of Communication – Networking, socializing, writing, speaking, teaching, intelligence, siblings, local travel, early childhood environment

4th House of Home & Family – Mother, caretaker, home, ancestry, heritage, roots, early foundation/environment, nurturing self and others

5th House – House of Pleasure: Fun, leisure activities, children, love, romance, creative self-expression, sex, entertainment, games and gambling

6th House of Health – Routine tasks, duties, jobs, employment, training, skills, health and overall wellbeing, caretaking, pets, service performed for others

7th House of Partnerships – Close relationships, marriage, business partners, agreements, diplomatic relations, attraction of qualities we admire in others, collaboration

8th House of Reincarnation – Cycles of death and rebirth, inheritance, committed relationships, joint finances, taboo, regeneration, self-transformation

9th House of Philosophy – Culture, foreign travels, religion, law and ethics, higher education, knowledge, expansion through experiences, higher learning

10th House of Social Status – Ambitions, motivation, career, status, government, authority, father figure, breadwinner, public appearance or impressions, wealth,

11th House of Friendship – Friends, acquaintances, like-minded groups, clubs, higher associations, benefits and fortunes from career, hopes and wishes

12th House of Self-Undoing – Mysticism, mystery, places of seclusion such as hospitals, prisons including self-imposed imprisonments, things which are not apparent to us, unconscious/subconscious, unknown enemies, karma, secrets

About the Author

Jana Groscost lives in Pismo Beach, California. She is a metaphysical teacher, healer, speaker, and writer. She integrates mindfulness philosophies into personal and business development programs. As a former tax accountant, she combines traditional business practices with spiritual principles, providing heart-centered entrepreneurs tools and information about consciously expanding their business. Her passion is in **enlightening minds, expanding hearts, and empowering souls** so people learn how to manifest whatever they want. Get connected:

Facebook Groups – facebook.com/NewMoonManifesting
Facebook Groups - facebook.com/ManifestingEssentials
http://www.NewMoonManifesting.com
http://www.ManifestingEssentials.com
Google Plus - plus.google.com/+ManifestingEssentials/
Twitter - twitter.com/JanaGroscost

Additional Personal Notes

Made in the USA
Middletown, DE
26 January 2017